HEALING THE BODY, STRETCHING THE MIND . . .

☆

Edgar Cayce's Medical Readings helped many people regain their health as well as acquire a different perspective on life. Cayce's treatments evolved from viewing the body as a physical-mental-spiritual entity. His therapies, combining diet, nutrition, and psychic aspects, often challenged traditional Western medicine and anticipated the contemporary holistic health movement by decades. The fate of the people who received these Medical Readings and the findings of modern medicine since Cayce's time that confirm the effectiveness of Cayce's therapies make for fascinating, provocative reading. And his radical, revolutionary approaches to healing for both common and uncommon ailments can offer new hope and new possibilities for people today.

☆

EDGAR CAYCE ON HEALING

Books in
The Edgar Cayce Series

THERE WILL YOUR HEART BE ALSO
DREAMS YOUR MAGIC MIRROR
EDGAR CAYCE ON DIET AND HEALTH
EDGAR CAYCE ON HEALING
DREAMS IN THE LIFE OF PRAYER
EDGAR CAYCE ON RELIGION AND
PSYCHIC EXPERIENCE
EDGAR CAYCE ON ESP
THE EDGAR CAYCE READER
EDGAR CAYCE ON ATLANTIS
THE EDGAR CAYCE READER #2
EDGAR CAYCE ON DREAMS
EDGAR CAYCE ON PROPHECY
EDGAR CAYCE ON REINCARNATION
EDGAR CAYCE ON JESUS AND HIS CHURCH
EDGAR CAYCE ON THE DEAD SEA SCROLLS
EDGAR CAYCE ENCYCLOPEDIA OF HEALING
EDGAR CAYCE ON MYSTERIES OF THE MIND*
YOU CAN REMEMBER YOUR PAST LIVES*
EDGAR CAYCE ON THE POWER OF COLOR, STONES, AND CRYSTALS*
EDGAR CAYCE ANSWERS LIFE'S
10 MOST IMPORTANT QUESTIONS*
EDGAR CAYCE ON THE SECRETS OF THE UNIVERSE*

Published by
WARNER BOOKS

*forthcoming

EDGAR CAYCE
ON
HEALING

BY MARY ELLEN CARTER AND
WILLIAM A. McGAREY, M.D.
UNDER THE EDITORSHIP OF
HUGH LYNN CAYCE

WARNER BOOKS

A Warner Communications Company

WARNER BOOKS EDITION

Cover design by Gene Light

Warner Books, Inc.
666 Fifth Avenue
New York, N.Y. 10103

A Warner Communications Company

Printed in the United States of America

First Warner Books Printing: May, 1972

Reissued: October, 1988

15   14   13   12   11

Contents

Foreward *by Hugh Lynn Cayce* 7

Introduction *by William A. McGarey, M.D.* 11

Personal Narratives by Mary Ellen Carter and Medical Commentaries by William A. McGarey, M.D.

1. The Lady Who Was Turning To Stone 19

   Medical Commentary: Scleroderma 32

2. A Friend, Snatched From Death 42

   Medical Commentary: Streptococcus 49

3. A Mother's Ordeal 58

   Medical Commentary: Incoordination 67

4. The Turning Point 76

   Medical Commentary: Peritonitis, Gangrene 85

5. Grandmother Takes A Hand 91

   Medical Commentary: Ear Infection 96

6. Tell Them The Lame Walk 103

Medical Commentary: Perthe's Disease 111

7. No Surgery For Ken! 120

Medical Commentary: Appendicitis 124

8. Teen-Age Arthritic 132

Medical Commentary: Appendicitis 124

9. For Leonore, "The Glory" 150

Medical Commentary: Infertility 156

10. Maytime Malady 163

Medical Commentary: Debilitation 170

11. Call This A Miracle 175

Medical Commentary: Cerebral Palsy 181

12. For Life Itself Is A Service 187

Medical Commentary: Paralysis 197

The A. R. E. Today 204

Foreword

The twentieth-century history of parapsychology will probably catalogue Edgar Cayce, one of America's best-documented psychics, as a medical telepathist. The Association for Research and Enlightenment, Inc., a psychical research society, was formed in 1932 to preserve and experiment with his data. Its library in Virginia Beach, Virginia contains 14,246 copies of Edgar Cayce's psychic readings, stenographically recorded over a period of 43 years. Of this number 8,976, or about 64%, describe the physical disabilities of several thousand persons and suggest treatment for their ailments.

For a great many physicians, medical studies of treatment patterns for a number of major physical diseases seem to suggest the advisability of testing Edgar Cayce's theories. With this in mind, the physical readings have been made available to a clinic in Phoenix, Arizona staffed by four medical doctors. Through written reports and yearly conferences, information on results of treatments are being made available to more than 250 M.D.'s and osteopaths.

After two years of clinical work with the readings and ten years of study and testing in private practice, William McGarey, M.D., Director of the A.R.E. Clinic in Phoenix, agreed to collaborate with Mary Ellen Carter, a long time A.R.E. member and widely-known author on Edgar Cayce data, in bringing to print the human interest stories of a selection of original readings given by Edgar Cayce. For each one, Dr. McGarey has added an up-to-date medical commentary. Many of our readers have heard these stories told; here at last are the exciting details.

For some of you, this may be the first introduction to Edgar Cayce. Who was he?

It depends on through whose eyes you look at him. A goodly number of his contemporaries knew the "waking" Edgar Cayce as a gifted professional photographer. Another group (predominantly children) admired him as a warm and friendly Sunday School teacher. His own family knew him as a wonderful husband and father.

The "sleeping" Edgar Cayce was an entirely different figure—a psychic known to thousands of people from all walks of life who had cause to be grateful for his help. Indeed, many of them believed that he alone had either saved or changed their lives when all seemed lost. The "sleeping" Edgar Cayce was a medical diagnostician, a prophet, and a devoted proponent of Bible lore.

Even as a child on a farm near Hopkinsville, Kentucky, where he was born on March 18, 1877, Edgar Cayce displayed powers of perception which seemed to extend beyond the normal range of the five senses. At the age of six or seven he told his parents that he was able to see and talk to "visions," sometimes of relatives who had recently died. His parents attributed this to the overactive imagination of a lonely child who had been influenced by the dramatic language of the revival meetings which were popular in that section of the country. Later, by sleeping with his head on his schoolbooks, he developed some form of photographic memory which helped him advance rapidly in the country school. This gift faded, however, and Edgar was only able to complete his seventh grade before he had to go to work.

By the age of twenty-one he had become the salesman for a wholesale stationery company. At this time he developed a gradual paralysis of the throat muscles, which threatened to cause the loss of his voice. When doctors were unable to find a physical cause for this condition, hypnosis was tried but failed to have any permanent effect. As a last resort Edgar asked a friend to help him re-enter the same kind of hypnotic sleep that had enabled him to memorize his schoolbooks as a child. His friend gave him the necessary suggestion, and once he was in a self-induced trance, Edgar came to grips with his own problem. Speaking from an unconscious state, he recommended medication and manipulative therapy which successfully restored his voice and repaired his system.

A group of physicians from Hopkinsville and Bowling Green, Kentucky took advantage of his unique talent to diagnose their own patients. They soon discovered that Cayce needed to be given only the name and address of a patient, wherever he was, to be able to tune in telepathically to that individual's mind and body as easily as if they were both in the same room. He needed no other information regarding any patient.

One of the young M.D.'s, Dr. Wesley Ketchum, submitted a report on this unorthodox procedure to a clinical research society in Boston. On October 9, 1910, *The New York Times* carried two pages of headlines and pictures. From that day on troubled people from all over the country sought help from the "wonder man."

When Edgar Cayce died on January 3, 1945, in Virginia Beach, Virginia, he left the previously mentioned 14,000 documented stenographic records of the telepathic-clairvoyant statements he had given for more than 6000 different people over a period of 43 years. These readings constitute one of the largest and most impressive records of psychic perception ever to emanate from a single individual. Together with their relevant records, correspondence and reports, they have been cross-indexed under thousands of subject headings and placed at the disposal of psychologists, physicians, students, writers and investigators who still come, in increasing numbers, to examine them.

As an open-membership research, the Association continues to index and catalog the information, initiate investigation and experiments and promote conferences, seminars and lectures. Until the initiation of this paperback series, its published findings were made available only to its members through its own publishing facilities.

—Hugh Lynn Cayce

CASES CURED IN THE CAYCE READINGS

Introduction

This book is about a psychic and his work in suggesting methods by which healing might come to the human body. These suggestions centered on the field of medicine and spread out over osteopathy, chiropractic, physical therapy, herbal therapy, nutrition, spiritual therapy, hypnotherapy, dentistry, and what is best described as "other methods." As a waking individual, Edgar Cayce often looked into the future in flashes of insight or, at times, viewed a person's makeup from the appearance of his aura and commented on it, apparently seeing events in the past and in the future which dealt with that person's total life as an individual. His psychic ability was indeed unique while he was in the full waking state.

Asleep, however, Cayce apparently found the curtains pulled widely apart which for most of us usually obscure the past, the future, and the true nature of man as seen in the skein of time and space. He found himself giving information that, in his own unconscious state, he termed as arising from universal sources. He described events of the future with almost as great a clarity as he discussed the physiological functioning of an ailing human body that might be 2,000 miles away. In this state he apparently had communication with the unconscious minds of people everywhere but specifically with the mind of that person for whom he was giving a reading. Much has been written about this in numerous publications, and he has been adjudged the outstanding sensitive of the twentieth-century.

All of this activity at the unconscious level still allowed him to dream and, upon awakening from a reading, he was able to describe the dream experience. Even the dream, Cayce suggests, is a psychic experience which often participates in the past and the future and predicts for those who would study their dreams every important event destined to happen in their lives. Many important personal as well as world prophecies came to Cayce in dreams, both during the course of a reading and at the more normal dream times—at night while he slept.

At times during a reading, he would correct the shorthand notes made by his secretary who was sitting across the room and who had made an error in transcription of a word or a phrase. His mind, indeed, had many facets. and he has, after his death, become an object of study by interested researchers from many fields of scientific endeavor.

His discussion of an individual's travel through time led to the interweaving through all of the Cayce material of that theory which is called reincarnation, or the continuity of a soul's existence through all time.

His work with illnesses of the human body has provided for me the most fascinating and potentially important information that I have found in the 14,500 readings he gave over a period of some 40 years. Some 9,000 of these readings dealt with human illness and its correction.

The manner in which he was able to describe conditions with such accuracy—illnesses and points of strength of which he had no conscious awareness—has within it implications that are not easily avoided to all those involved in the field of healing.

Since I enjoy a challenge, and since the nature of a researcher demands an open mind, this material then became a most exciting experience for me. It has gradually suggested the possibility that we, in our present state of knowledge and understanding, are far removed from the perfect comprehension of this amazing creation that we call the human body.

I realize that most physicians do not relish the idea of commenting publicly on the validity of psychic data —especially when this is dealt with in depth. But then most medical doctors have never either studied or experienced psychic happenings. Aside from the dream world, which most of us do not consider to be dealing with any manner of what is called ESP, we as physicians tend to stay away from the psychic event—especially in the practice of medicine—since it is so difficult to pin down with the current methodology of science. Also, if the truth be known, it scares us a bit.

When reincarnation with its concept of rebirth and karma—the law of cause and effect—is added to the picture, the gap for the physician then often grows wider. However, one studying the Cayce material must at some point deal with these concepts of the unusual qualities of the mind and the destiny of the soul as a timeless voyager in putting to rest the unique phenomenon that Mr. Cayce presents to us in his life and experiences.

Physicians with an oriental background do not have as much of a problem with the psychic as do occidentals, since the reality of the soul's voyage in continuity through many lifetimes is a portion of their heritage. Most orientals have accepted reincarnation as factual and not worth arguing about. This concept, they say, once accepted leads one away from a materialistic viewpoint and makes it easier to understand and accept psychic events and their implications.

Westerners for the most part are Judeo-Christian in their religious roots. There really should be no difficulty in accepting and understanding, to an extent, those things which we currently call "psychic" or what Shafica Karagulla, M.D., has called "higher sense perception." These religious teachings, based on the writings of the ancient Jews, are rich in psychic events. These include stories—often considered symbolic—such as Adam hearing God's words reverberating through a forest; the passage of the children of Israel through the divided Red Sea guided by an angel and a pillar of cloud by day and a pillar of fire by night; Elijah's restoring a boy's life at the behest of his mother; the dreams of Mary, Joseph, and the wise men guiding events in the life of the baby Jesus; healings of many kinds of afflictions by Jesus and his disciples; and the revelation of John, who did not know whether he was "in the spirit" or not—but saw some of the same symbols described much earlier by Ezekiel, Jeremiah, and other Old Testament prophets.

Cayce's work, then, poses somewhat of a problem for those of us who are physicians and claim to be Jewish or Christian in our belief. For we can deny believing psychic things only at the expense of divesting ourselves of some of our most precious religious concepts. To be a Jew or a Christian and to say that the psychic world is a myth is to introduce confusion into our methods of thinking and thus into our lives as a whole.

The Bible presents man as a spiritual being who is in that manner like unto God. Man as a physical creation with a mind capable of creative activity, even to the extent of denying his Creator, does not detract from his spiritual origin and existence. This spiritual reality, described rather explicitly in the Bible, is the basis—as Edgar Cayce sees man—for his inherent ability to perform in a manner which we call psychic. Thus, Cayce presents a

14

challenge, not only to the physician—although he is perhaps primarily involved as far as this book is concerned—but to every reader, to evaluate the factual material which is present in the readings and to look at it with the degree of honesty and open mindedness that scientists must use in approaching a research problem.

This might lead one, then, to accept the implications in this mass of data and understand man's psychic capabilities as a part of one's daily life. Cayce would suggest that this then would bring all events of one's life into perspective as they relate to the activity of the soul and would lead one to see all events of life—even illness—as a necessary and perhaps a learning experience as man passes through time and space.

Leaving supposition, implication, philosophy, and other imponderables aside, I should point out that this book is written consistently in two parts. In the major structure of the writing, Mary Ellen Carter has created a picture of factual data revolving around the lives of several people (some critically ill) and who, through suggestions given by Mr. Cayce in his sleep-state, regained their health as well as a different perspective on life. The information in these stories is factual, and the details can be found in the library of the Association for Research and Enlightenment. People were interviewed, stories were substantiated, and the material from the readings was deliberately drawn upon to unfold the events in these people's lives.

Mrs. Carter has attempted to portray in these stories the human events that take place within a home and a family as sickness of a serious nature strikes. The doubts, the confusions that come about as people seek to find healing for their bodies in different manners is for each person, perhaps, a time of crisis in his life experience. For these same doubts and confusions and what one does about them may indeed shape and color one's total life accomplishments. These people are like most of us. They, however, asked for information from a source most people at the time considered to be really "way out"—a source that just could not be truly understood. For most people of that day, Cayce's information just "did not compute."

Each of Mrs. Carter's accounts is followed by a discussion of the physiological concepts and the various therapeutic modalities which Cayce suggested and which were then a part of these various lives. I have tried to be factual and objective in my approach while adding to the discussion the concepts which seem to evolve out of this psychic data concerning the manner in which the human body functions, its nature as a physical-mental-spiritual entity, and the therapeutic approach which should be made to restore a body from a state of illness to its natural condition of health. I have drawn rather heavily on quotations from pertinent readings which illustrate how Cayce's concepts of man and his existence here on the earth vary from our present understanding of the body and utilization of therapy in treating disease.

I hope you enjoy reading this as much as I have enjoyed participating in writing it.

William A. McGarey, M.D.

All names have been changed except those of the Cayce family and their friends as they are mentioned; the Cayce Hospital Staff members; Mrs. Gladys Davis Turner, secretary to Edgar Cayce; and several doctors and practical nurses who are indicated by an asterisk.

M.E.C.

Chapter I

The Lady Who Was Turning To Stone

Disaster often overtakes us like a cat that steals upon its prey. For Florence Evans, 29, organist and choir director for the Toddesville Methodist Church on that chill November evening in 1937, the cat was about to spring.

She paused as she started up the church steps. There were only three of them, and yet her knees seemed to buckle a little and there was a strange shortness of breath accompanied by profuse perspiration in the palms of her hands. "I must be coming down with the flu again," she thought and swung the heavy door open with an effort.

Sunday's service was an ordeal for her. She was hardly able to play the hymns, the special anthem seemed to her to drag interminably, and the postlude was agony. At the end of the service she was aching throughout her body, perspiring, and near collapse. She managed to get herself out to her parents' Ford parked at the side of the church, and there she stayed until they came out to find her.

They rushed her home to the little house on Maple Street and put her to bed. She was so hot inside, she complained. And she wanted some aspirin!

After a day, when she was still in bed and had not improved, Dr. Harold Maddox was called in. He was certain, he said, that Florence had the flu. "Let her drink plenty of liquids, keep her in bed, and have her take the medicine I'll send around."

Every day she tried to get up; but the unrelenting ache engulfed her now, and she would fall back exhausted into bed.

Christmas came and went, and still she grew no better. Ten days before Christmas, she noticed an odd hardening of the flesh on her hips. "It's because I'm lying around so much," she thought. "I'm getting bedsores."

But the hardening grew worse. One day, she found that her flesh was hard throughout her body from her hips down to her knees.

By now, she had been examined by three doctors, all of whom were baffled by her symptoms.

Like a fresh breeze was her Aunt Stacy who lived in another town close by and who was her mother's sister. She was a tall, independent-minded soul who had married rather late in life and was not at all apologetic about it. Now she came swooping in upon the scene with a firm hand.

"Cara," said Aunt Stacy to her mother, "you are to get some sleep. You will let me make some of the decisions, and you are to let me help you with the housework. And, of course, I can nurse Florence as well as anybody."

Florence was taken by her mother and father to Nashville in January to enter the Haggard Clinic for tests. It was just after New Year's, the weather was cold, the trip dreary. When the tests were over, they assured her, they would know what to do.

But after all the examinations were done, the doctor who had greeted them now gave them little encouragement. Florence had a hardening and thickening of the skin, which they called "derma," or scleroderma.

"There have been only 400 cases like yours on record," Florence's father told her later. It was several days before Florence was told that very few such cases ever recovered.

"Florence Evans, the lady who's turning to stone," she thought as she lay in bed in her own room once more. It was a nightmare! One of pain and unnatural change through which she had been living for eight weeks. She had been pretty: grey eyes and chestnut hair. Now, when she looked into a mirror, the face of a stranger stared back at her, swollen and rigid. And it was hard, like her hips, now.

And the unspeakable word which no one had used, but which everybody understood, had filtered into her consciousness: the word *incurable*.

On January 6, Dr. Maddox came to visit her and said that he would obtain some information from a research laboratory about Florence's condition. Now her hopes soared, for she had faith in the science of her day. She still clung to the thought that some magic would be found to work for her.

But two days later, she awoke with the aching permeating her body more than ever, compounded by a burning sensation along her spine. Her mother came in, bringing aspirin and water. She took them gratefully, carefully propping herself up with a contrived smile. Her father came in and sat down on a chair by the bed.

"Florence, have you forgotten Cayce?" he asked, his head tilted inquisitively, his lean face gentle.

She was suddenly aware of the sun pouring into her room. And aware, too, more than she dared to admit even to herself, of her faith that a reading from Edgar Cayce, the clairvoyant "doctor" of Virginia Beach, would be the answer to her desperate need.

She was well informed of the unorthodox treatments he usually prescribed. She knew, also, that he had read for hundreds of people right there in Toddesville and the surrounding community, as well as people in many parts of the country. When medical doctors had failed, or found nothing could be done for their patients, Cayce had been called in to give readings, although he remained in his home miles away! Miraculous results had followed his diagnoses and treatments given for many people, and his fame was growing every day.

Three years ago she herself had been advised by him in a reading to "purify" her body by taking internally doses of a weird concoction containing essence of wild cherry, essence of poke-root, essence of yellow dock root, and several other ingredients. She had had to change her diet quite drastically, too: no fried foods, but a lot of fresh vegetables; no pork and not much beef; no bananas and no ice cream. But she had overcome her case of acne, and it had taken a mere seven or eight months.

Thinking back over that experience and recalling, too, that her mother, father, and Aunt Stacy all had had readings by Edgar Cayce that proved beneficial, she began to smile.

Her father said, "That's better!"

And her mother wept quietly as she sat at the foot of the bed. When Aunt Stacy was told on the telephone of the message they planned to send to Cayce that very day, she said, "*Now* we'll see some action!"

"Yes," began Forence's reading given a few days later, "we have the body here. This we have had before. As we find, it has been rather late in beginning with the disturbances that have arisen. . . ."

He went on to say that the disturbances were of a very subtle nature and that unless there could be something to help resist the inroads of a *tubercle* in Florence's body, the condition would rapidly become worse. He suggested that the tubercle was making inroads in the respiratory system and the muscles, as well as the red blood cells.

To throw off these conditions, castor oil packs should be applied over the abdominal area and also the lower part of the back up to the diaphragm. Also, Ventriculin in small quantity should be taken twice daily. She should have beef juice often and little or no starchy foods.

Specific details as to quantities and times were given for the application of these treatments. The packs, to begin immediately, were to be continued "until there has been stayed this tendency for the formation of knots or clots by the blood supply attempting to make for coagulations; and thus forming in the muscular forces, and drainings upon the system at the same time, those hardened places—not only in the spinal area, but in the abdominal area, also . . ."

The reading was translated later that very day into the following telegram, which Florence read with great elation as she sat propped up in bed: "Sponge off with saturated solution bicarbonate of soda, then apply hot castor oil packs heavy over abdomen and lower spine for three hours. Rest three hours, begin again. Also take Ventriculin without iron half teaspoonful twice daily. Small quantities pure beef juice often with Ry-Krisp or whole wheat crackers. No other breads or starches. Use enemas body temperature rather than cathartics. Full information special. Consult Mrs. Stacia Holms for immediate application suggestions."

"Mrs. Stacia Holms" was, of course, Aunt Stacy, and she was delighted to supervise the treatments. She had nursed many of her relatives and friends as a practical nurse, and she was a welcomed presence now.

She stood silently by the door in the room and with Cara and Paul Evans listened while Florence read the telegram aloud. When she had finished, Stacy thumped the night stand. "I *knew* Cayce would know!" she exulted. "Let's start right in!"

"What do we do first?" Cara said breathlessly.

"We have to get a lot of castor oil," observed Paul quietly.

Florence giggled.

"Yes. And a box of bicarbonate of soda, and that Ventriculin from the drug store . . . without iron . . . Oh, I must write down a list!"

"We'll need a big piece of oil cloth," said Stacy.

When Paul returned a little later with the items on Cara's list, Stacy expertly began the ritual of bathing Florence's body with the soda solution and then enveloping her in hot castor oil packs. Florence took her first dose of Ventriculin. They entered the treatment with rejoicing. Florence sensed that Stacy was going about her work, not mechanically, but as if she were indeed in league with the Higher Forces. Once, Florence would have seen no connection between scientific application of healing agents, and God. Now she told Stacy, "We're working with God!"

A little later, she looked up to see that Stacy's eyes were closed, as if in prayer. Florence said nothing, but closed her eyes and raised her own thoughts to ascend with those being offered up on her behalf. It proved to be a moment in which together they shared a healing Presence. Florence was to cling to that moment in the months to come.

"I've never had such a case before," Stacy told Paul later in the hallway, out of Florence's hearing, "nor seen such a pitiful condition. Frankly, it's going to be a long, uphill work."

The temperature and sweating which Florence was experiencing were due to the tubercle, said the reading which arrived in its entirety a few days later. This germ had attacked the blood stream. Florence was to remain in bed, yet she was to have "plenty of fresh air" in her room. Fumes from Oil of Pine burned in the room would help her chest as would fumes from equal portions of Eucalyptol and Tincture of Benzoin.

Five days after beginning the treatment, color was reappearing in Florence's face. Her mother wrote Edgar Cayce, "I thank you so much for your interest in us and pray that there is some help for her. . ."

Always, Stacy seemed to apply the packs with a loving

24

prayer in which Florence found it natural that she herself participate. With Cara, it was more verbal: "Oh, Father, please make our little girl well." She often said it at bedtime, just as she had when Florence was small.

But with Stacy, she *was* the prayer. She uttered it in her very step, in the way she put her head on one side and sized up a person or a situation from her own secret vantage point. Her strong hands moved through the myriad of services for her patient like the hands of a devout woman making the sign of the Cross or folding in prayer. There was about her a healing force that emanated to all who met her.

A few days after they removed the packs from Florence's regimen, they were dismayed to discover that she was becoming worse. On a Sunday evening, they sat near her bed, contemplating her plight. Florence lay with her eyes closed, her face pale, her body limp with fatigue. She had to be propped up on pillows to get her breath.

They decided to call Dr. Maddox, because she was becoming distraught with the agony in her chest. When he arrived, he had little to say as he examined her. But he offered no hope and said merely, "Watch her carefully. I will be at home tonight and in my office tomorrow." He went out into the hall.

Then he added, "I'm sorry," to Cara and Paul. Paul nodded because there was nothing to say.

After he had left, Cara wept against Paul's shoulder. "She's dying!"

Stacy silently began to get out the castor oil and the oilcloth. Later, as Florence remained about the same though she was wrapped in the pack, they seemed to be back where they had started.

They decided to seek another reading from Cayce at once. Stacy insisted, "Don't send for this unless you are going to follow it!"

Injections given by the doctor had "caused disturbances

25

to the heart's activity, to the coordination between the sympathetic and the cerebro-spinal system," said this reading.

The oil packs had been obtaining results, since they had been properly given. They were to be kept up now for several days at a time, then stopped for a rest period of a week. All other phases of the therapy were to be continued, particularly the starchless diet.

One new kind of treatment was added: application of a low electrical vibration by means of the "wet cell appliance" described by Cayce in previous readings for other illnesses. Substances which would be added to her body by this means would be Atomidine, Chloride of Gold, and Spirits of Camphor. The daily treatments would last for thirty minutes each. Cayce described how to make the attachments in detail: the plates were to be attached to various parts of Florence's body to allow the different solutions to impart their beneficial influences.

"Each solution carries to the circulation the vibrations of these properties to act upon the glandular system, as well as the circulation," said the reading.

For ten days she used the wet cell appliance as directed. There was never any sensation except that of well-being. Secretly, she wondered if the thing could really help her. Just as the packs were deceptively simple, so, too, were the low electrical vibrations that produced simply a pleasant relaxation and a predisposition to sleep.

Then, unaccountably, she experienced a rigor accompanied by severe aching. There was bleeding from the rectum. Another occurred, and she wired Cayce to ask if she was using the appliance correctly.

This was, she was told, "the system's attempting to adjust itself and eliminate those disturbances in the circulation that have caused the checking of the flow to the lymph circulation." The rigors arose from the attempts of her body to throw off the poisons in her system.

Changes were made in treatment. Alcohol rubs were added, and advice was given to continue with enemas using Glyco-Thymoline. It was now spring. Florence remained very ill, although improvement was noticeable.

On March 5, her mother wrote Cayce that Florence was not well and that her stomach trouble was something new. Strangely, on that very day Cayce volunteered a reading for Florence at the end of another person's physical check reading after Hugh Lynn Cayce, as conductor, had given the suggestion, "That is all."

Began this unsolicited advice: "Now the conditions are much on the improve, by the vibrations that have been set up through the system by the low electrical forces and the rub," and he identified this reading as being for Florence Evans, Toddesville, Kentucky!

"These should be kept," he went on. He gave further directions for the use of the wet cell and added that a charred keg of a gallon and a half be half-filled with pure apple brandy and that the fumes from this, heated, might be "inhaled whenever there is the tendency for a shaky or ague feeling or weakness."

Wrote Cara in reply: "The reading . . . was an answer to my prayers. We are so very grateful to you for this information. She has been so bright and cheerful all day. We felt that in some ways her condition was improved, yet she suffers so much from the aching. The hardness of her skin is less, though very evident yet, through the hips and limbs to knees. May God bless you and your wonderful work. . ."

There had been a turning point. Her next reading now shifted from strictly physical healing to a high level of spiritual attitudes, particularly to be assumed during the wet cell treatments. Then she should be "in a meditative, prayerful mind," putting herself "into the hands, into the arms, into the care of the Savior. Not merely as trusting, not merely as hoping, but as relying upon the promises. And make them cooperative, co-active. Be used for something, not only good but good for something, that ye may bring into the experience of others—even by thine own ability to suffer—the glorious knowledge of the work-

27

ing of the Christ-Consciousness within the individual mind. . ."

"For if these are adhered to," stated this reading, "if these are kept, we will find the helpful forces in every manner; not only with the patience to bear the cross of distress or anxiety but with the means and the friends and the hopes to *carry on* for Him!"

By May, she had improved so much that the hardness was disappearing, her temperature was normal, and there were no more night sweats. But because she still suffered with the aching, she decided to go to the Mayo Clinic for tests and left off the castor oil packs once more. Soon she was suffering again with rigors and temperature, as well as the sweats. Now another reading put her back on the packs and other aids. In time her health returned to the point where she wanted to go back to her work of teaching music and conducting her choir.

In her next reading she asked, "Will you please tell me if you can when I can go back to work and if I should work at the church and teach also?"

She was told that she should do both. "These are a part of [your]self." She was to "Keep the constructive forces in much of the prayer and meditation, and especially in the periods when the appliance is used. Raise that vibration within self that there are within self the healing forces. For all healing of every nature comes only from the One Source, the Giver of all good and perfect gifts."

She was free now from the necessity of using the daily packs and was to take them only when she had a spell of "rigors." She was to use instead gentle olive oil rubs.

Cara was afraid she would pull her health down by going back to work. "Well, maybe Cayce can get me in such good health that I won't have any flu this winter," Florence told her.

Her aunt had gone home long before now, and when Florence told her the news that she was going back to work, Stacy was equally exuberant. "Don't get too frisky," she warned. "You're not out of the woods yet."

"I know. But just to get out of those packs is like heaven! In this heat they're not very funny."

But even at the end of summer the aching did not leave her. "It's setting me wild," she reported to Cayce in late July.

She wrote him in August, "When I was taken with this trouble, the doctors called it flu. That was before we found the hardness, though. I was taken the same way as I have been with every spell of flu. I sometimes wonder if it hasn't been this trouble coming on for a long time. Would the flu shots do me any good? I would do anything to escape it. I dread the first cold spell until spring."

She was not to take flu shots, said her subsequent reading. She was to take halibut oil with Viosterol to help build muscular forces and to work with the enzymes in the Ventriculin. She was now for the first time to take osteopathic treatments: massage, rather than manipulation, however. If she was tired or weak or in pain, she was to have an oil pack followed by general massage. The electrical therapy was to be administered once a day or so.

The first Friday night in September she returned to her beloved choir. She opened the big heavy church door and walked into a waiting group that hugged her and congratulated her.

On the first Sunday morning, as she played the organ once again and led the choir and congregation through the musical part of the service, she was so nervous that she almost jumped up and ran from the choir loft. Members of the congregation could not resist coming up and speaking to her after church. She still ached with pain in her shoulders; and if she moved her head, it was worse. It was difficult now for her to speak with these well-wishers, but she made the effort, despite the perspiration that formed in her palms.

During the days of her recovery, Edgar Cayce wrote to her about a young girl who had been told in a life reading that she should play the organ. She lived right there in Toddesville and would Florence teach her, if he, Cayce, paid for the lessons?

Florence wrote him that she would be very happy to, and "I can't take money from you after what you have done for me. I'll never make enough money to pay you; in fact, money can't pay you for helping me the way you have."

Throughout the winter she persisted in the treatments which gradually led her to full recovery. By May she was considered fully cured except for a neuritic condition. Cayce now told her she was working too hard, and he said (in her reading) "Rest sufficiently, play sufficiently, work sufficiently—but think constructively!"

He was cognizant of her problems now with her new life, and had advice to heal and to nourish the soul, as well as the body: "Take into consideration more often the purposes of the activities, not as the outward appearances in thy choir practice but what do such activities stand for? What is the message that is to be given to the world through this channel of singing? The love of the Christ to the world!

"Then let it be a personal thing to thee, that He is thy strength, He is thy life! For in Him ye live and move and have thy being.

"There is too much work and too much worry to the amount of play and relaxation . . . Better divide it up! Did you find the Master worked continually or did He take time to play? And time to relax? He is a good example in *everyone's* life."

* * *

Florence Evans later completed her musical education, obtaining her Bachelor of Music degree. She married and has established herself as a very busy organist and choir director for three churches. She has only dim memories now of her long fight for life. She had once told her mother, "I won't stop fighting 'til I get well." And she didn't. The aching has long since gone, and she is completely well.

"People think I'm a curiosity," she once wrote to Hugh Lynn Cayce. She has smilingly told many people that she would have died if it hadn't been for Edgar Cayce. So it isn't surprising that she added in the same letter: "A girl from —— came to see me . . . She is so pitiful with a different form of scleroderma from mine. The doctors at Vanderbilt Hospital in Nashville are at their 'row's end.' I told her how I was cured. I hope she will be as persistent as I was in the treatment if she gets a reading . . ."

Medical Commentary: Scleroderma

by William A. McGarey, M.D.

In order to understand Mr. Cayce's approach to sclero-derma as well as to any particular disease process, it would be well to establish some guidelines and principles as they are derived from the readings that Cayce himself gave from the unconscious state. These principles would be applicable in a discussion of all of the stories in this book—so they need be presented only once.

Cayce looks at the human being as a three-dimensional manifestation of a spiritual reality. He recognizes that we are in fact composed basically of atoms which are units of force and energy, and he attributes the quality of consciousness to these basic structural units. Thus he states, in effect, that man as we know him is composed of energy which is in a state of homeostasis, a balance and coordination that forms a structure which we can see and feel. This, of course, is in accord with present-day understanding of the atom—with the exception perhaps that we in the field of science have not yet attributed to the atom a specific consciousness. We do, however, see the oxygen atom as "doing its thing" quite differently from the iron atom, for instance. Perhaps Mr. Cayce is not too far afield even in that regard.

The body, then, from the Cayce viewpoint, is a unit made up of billions of cells, each with a consciousness, and each being composed in turn of billions of atoms, each of these also being points of consciousness or awareness of a type. All these, in their sum total and in their relationship with each other, make up the greater awareness which we individually call "I."

Cayce would have us believe that groups of cells—which we know as organs and systems—act as separate forces within the body which must coordinate with each other in their activity in a balanced homeostasis in order that we may experience what we call health.

Disturbance of these forces, then (in the viewpoint of the readings), creates the environment, the activities, and the imbalances or incoordinations which design the situations which we at the present time call disease.

On the other hand, a state of health within the human body is recovered when measures are taken which might encourage the gradual restoration of normal structure within cells themselves and a recovery of proper coordination between these activities, these energies—these forces, as Cayce would call them—which we call systems and organs of the body.

If the body is thus designed, as Cayce implies, a disease then is in the making when something in the structure and relationship of the body-mind-soul unit becomes unbalanced or disturbed. Order and balance must once again be established before health is fully present, and those external factors are eliminated which our present-day medical understanding considers to be the true etiology. It certainly becomes more evident in such a physical body that etiology and therapy are often quite closely related.

To add further to the fascination of the situation, and

33

perhaps also to the confusion, Cayce gave a number of readings which commented on the true nature of healing. Sometimes he related it to etiology or cause. The following extract from case 1472-14 was offered to explain why the administrations which were used for this individual who had sinus and digestive problems were not as effective as had been hoped.

This does not imply, then, that these are incurable; but, as is the influence in ALL healing, whether the administrations be purely suggestive, of a vibratory nature, from the laying on of hands, or by the spoken word, the administration of medicinal properties or even the use of means to remove diseased tissue, we find that the same source of individuality in the cause must be attained. That is, that which has been dissenting in its nature through the physical forces of the body must be so attuned to spiritual forces in itself as to become revitalized.

This then, as we have indicated, does not mean that NO condition cannot be improved, or that no condition cannot be healed.

As to what is that necessary influence to bring about curative or healing or life giving forces for that individuality and personality of the individual with same, as related to the spiritual forces, may be answered only within the individual itself. For, no source passes judgment. For, the spirituality, the individuality of the God-force in each entity's combined forces, must be its judge.

These preceding ideas, then, must be kept in mind if one desires to achieve an understanding of the position of the Cayce readings on: (1) the creative nature and the physiology of the human body and (2) the various factors and methods involved in producing a return to health.

We turn, then, to scleroderma and the story of Florence Evans, who was afflicted with one of the most severe manifestations of this disease—technically known as "progressive systemic sclerosis."

In today's medical-pathological understanding of this disease process, we find that scleroderma involves the collagenous connective tissues and may cause widespread symmetrical leathery induration of the skin followed by atrophy and pigmentation. The cutaneous lesions are believed to be the external manifestation of a systemic disease. The muscles, bones, mucous membranes, heart, lungs, intestinal tract, and other internal organs may be involved by the same process resulting in functional impairment such as heart failure or pulmonary insufficiency, and progressive, sometimes widespread organic pathology.

Its etiology is unknown. It may be related to other major connective tissue disorders, but the understanding of collagenous diseases is as yet incomplete.

The Cayce information describes scleroderma uniquely, using such concepts as coagulation, forces, and hardening of tissues. The autonomic nervous system becomes involved in the superficial circulation and its activities. Cayce describes how scleroderma affects not only the skin but also blood-forming structural areas such as bone and lung tissue in a process which produces a hardening or a clotting of the blood. This occurs mainly as a result of the blood attempting to bring about that creative activity which in the readings is called coagulation (the production of new cells as the old tissue normally dies.)

Cayce has described coagulation in rather poetic terms as creating cellular structure from energy—the energy supplied from several sources including molecules of food and oxygen assimilated into the body from the intestinal tract and the lungs. In scleroderma, this process is seen most dramatically hindered in the superficial capillaries and lymph vessels in the various layers of the skin. As these structures atrophy, the nerve endings locally become deadened. Cayce implies that this neurological involvement in Florence Evans' case produced acute pain in addition to a reflex activity directly involving the autonomic nervous system in the disease process. The impulses to the organ of the body from the sympathetic and parasympathetic nervous systems then became disturbed and uncoordinated. This, Cayce stated, led first to a disturbed state of function in the organs and finally to a pathological condition.

Hormone-producing cells in the thyroid, adrenals, and liver are deficient in supplying elements which aid in keeping the skin normal. These elements are, I would suppose, hormones, which this source of information states flatly are needed to maintain a normal degree of the coagulation process described earlier.

One might say that the glandular deficiency creates a lack of essential nutrition in the circulatory structures of the skin, which in turn causes a decrease in the lymph and capillary flow. As the disease progresses, the nerves in these areas become involved as described earlier, and a swelling then occurs in the skin as an attempt on the part of the body to bring about better conditions. As the lymph flow is destroyed, the lymphatics become inflamed and create the germ or the tubercle bacillus which "consumes" the circulation of the skin, forming a hardened area or placque. In the more advanced cases of scleroderma, the respiration of the skin also becomes involved . . . destruction of the sweat glands. Without the normal perspiration, a gradual increase in acidosis comes into being within the body, which then becomes more susceptible to colds and to intercurrent infections.

Nearly all portions of the body are involved in advanced cases of scleroderma, including the lungs. Increasing oxygen needs of the body can scarcely be met by a malfunctioning respiratory system, and the entire body is thus put under a greater strain. As these conditions progress, assimilation becomes more difficult and less capable, and the lack of reconstructive activities in the body becomes progressively more acute.

Review of the above information points to the understanding that the endocrine glands of the body in their disturbed functioning become the primary cause of this disease process, with the collagenous changes being secondary to the inadequate restoration of circulatory structures within the skin. The tubercle bacillus is in this instance a product of the body itself, not a secondary invader. A few medical theorists have implied that viruses derive sometimes from still vital chromosomal material left over from cellular breakdowns. But nowhere has the idea been proposed that the body may produce an acid-fast bacillus, or any type of bacteria, for that matter.

It is interesting to note that such bacilli were never discovered in the skin of scleroderma patients until some years after Cayce's death. In 1968 Cantwell[1] published a report on these findings and suggested that the acid-fast bacilli that he demonstrated might be the cause of scleroderma. This series of events has been interpreted—rightly, I believe—as valid medical clairvoyance of a very unusual type on the part of the sleeping Mr. Cayce.

In the therapy program which Cayce designed for Florence Evans throughout the course of many readings, one finds perhaps more questions than answers relative to mode of action that might be operative here. If Florence had not responded to Cayce's recommendations they could have then been dismissed. But she improved when she followed directions, worsened when she went off the therapy. It is uncanny to the practicing physician who must rely on his external powers of observation and what the laboratory facilities have to offer. It argues strongly that Cayce might indeed have been doing as he repeatedly said he did—actually communicating with the unconscious mind of the patient and relating while unconscious the state of affairs existing within that body. Even to the welfare of the individual red blood cells, or perhaps the blood forming organs.

[1] A. R. Cantwell, Jr., Eugenia Craggs, J. W. Wilson, and F. Swatek, "Acid-Fast-Bacteria as a Possible Cause of Scleroderma," *Dermatologica*, 136: 141–150.

Cayce's suggestions for Florence were almost legion in number. He seemed to view the body and its functions and abnormalities . . . reach into another psychic pocket, so to speak, and draw out a group of suggestions that would lead the ailing body back toward health, balancing these "forces" he spoke about so often and maintaining a homeostasis as it moved and changed.

Undoubtedly, in the case of scleroderma, Cayce saw so many systems and functions out of control that no therapy would be valuable unless it was designed to correct these functions in their relationship to each other. For instance, he frequently related the physiology of assimilation to that of elimination. He implied that adequate and normal assimilation of food taken into the upper intestinal tract cannot really come about unless the body is eliminating fully and normally. He also described the lymphatic system as part of the emunctory forces of the body, which puts the lymph then into the category of an eliminatory activity. The lymph nodes, then, no matter where they are found throughout the body, would necessarily be associated in some manner with elimination. Physiologically, of course, these comments have validity. The lymph does act as a drainage or eliminatory channel for individual cells and groups of cells throughout the body. The liver, which is the major detoxifier of the body, produces more lymph than any other single source.

Even with its "emunctory" activity, the lymph is also a part of the assimilatory apparatus of the body. We do not usually speak of assimilation today, but rather of digestion and metabolism. We are aware, however, that full assimilation means the process by which any substance is taken into the body and brought to its site of activity at the level of the cell. The many steps which are intermediary are all a part of this assimilatory process.

In the readings, it is also implied that in Florence's case the endocrine glands of the body as well as the blood were in a state that needed cleansing and purifying. He made suggestions as to how this would best be done.

But how would one understand the method by which the body is improved through the use of castor oil packs, for instance? What happens when soda is used to cleanse the skin first, and why does massage to the abdomen and to the back bring beneficial responses? What does Cayce mean by suggesting beef juice, for instance, or how valid is an alkaline diet? Why should grain alcohol massages bring more strength to the limbs and make for a better lymphatic circulation? Also, why should brandy fumes coming from a charred oak keg be so beneficial to the respiratory system of the body? What value to the body comes from a very, very low voltage electrical energy that is brought to the body through the medium of the wet cell battery Cayce devised?

These and other questions obviously come to one's mind as he reads the story of how Cayce's suggestions gradually nursed this young lady back to a full and healthy life.

Leaving specific therapy aside, we can see that the primary objective contained in the suggestions Cayce gave in his readings was the elimination of the basic cause of scleroderma—which has already been described as a malfunction of the glandular structures of the body. He suggested and emphasized the need for persistence and patience in gradually establishing a normal function throughout all those areas of the body which had been disturbed. Perhaps, then, we could safely say that the primary aim of Florence's therapy was the gradual redirecting of the forces and energies of the body back toward what we know and consider to be normal function.

The question of why these specific therapies work and whether they would again be effective at a clinical level would properly lie in the realm of medical research.

In looking at Florence Evans' story, one is struck by the fact that these applications which took so much time to become effective (in a condition as chronic and deep-set as scleroderma always is) required a persistence that often taxes the patience of anyone faced with this particular disease—whether it is the one who suffers or the one who applies therapy.

That Florence Evans had scleroderma is factual, certainly. She recovered completely over a period of time, using therapeutic modalities which seem to be a mixture of old-fashioned folk remedies and methods utilizing energies of the body the existence of which has not yet even been accepted. Cayce, in giving suggestions for therapy, implied, for instance, that the balance of the autonomic nervous system and its control of the circulation to the periphery of the body can be enhanced by the application of castor oil packs over the abdomen, extending around to cover the back. It is probably not just fortuitous that the coeliac (solar) plexus—the largest collection of nerve cells outside the brain—lies within the abdomen in that area. From material derived from the readings in various conditions of the body, it becomes evident that Cayce "saw" an effect on the nervous system from the application of such packs. How does this effect come about? Cayce speaks about vibratory influences in the reading I quoted earlier. The implication is there that all substances have an influence on the human body in a vibratory manner.

These vibratory effects, which are assumed throughout the Cayce readings to be active as beneficial or detrimental influences on the physical body, must be clearly differentiated from the biochemical and physical reactions which take place in the body. To understand such effects even partially, I would assume one would have to agree first that they play a part in the normal functioning of the body. One would also have to understand that there is much activity of an electrical nature going on in and about the body that we have not satisfactorily demonstrated at the present time. He would naturally have to agree that our present understanding of the body is only partial and incomplete and that much more is unknown than we presently know.

Perhaps these therapies Cayce suggested for Florence had their major effect on what he called the vibratory body. Such an idea would not be original with Cayce, of course. In fact, he stated outright that he derived his information from other minds or from the akashic record, or the Universal mind. Homeopathy deals with finer vibrations of the body. Acupuncturists see much in Cayce which coincides with their theories of a finer vibratory flow of energies through the body which connect various organs and systems in a manner that is not strictly neurological in its pathways. Treatment by the homeopaths is through the use of high dilutions of medicine taken into the body orally. The acupuncturist uses steel needles, usually wound at the hilt with gold, and inserts them into the skin at sites that have been found over the ages to be effective in changing the vibrational nature of the body in a constructive way.

Cayce himself described a flow of energy in the body which is in the shape of a figure of eight, with the lines crossing at the solar plexus. Other psychics have seen the same energy patterns. Individuals who have this clairvoyant gift see a higher vibrational body in addition to the physical body. If we allow that all these individuals are not consistently hallucinating, then the impact of this bit of information is that we must learn to deal with the vibrational nature of the body if we are really to make progress in the therapy of the human body and in understanding its true nature.

Florence Evans experienced, indeed, an unusual recovery from a disease which would otherwise have taken her life. My training in the field of medicine does not explain why or how this came about. Frustrating, isn't it?

"A Friend, Snatched From Death". . . .

by Mary Ellen Carter

"Roger McDermott, what's ailing you?" Bill Calhoun, eyes narrowed at his friend, challenged.

Roger shook his head. "Can't seem to get myself together," he replied. "Sorry I snapped at you. Beth's after me, too. Says I'm working too hard."

"Wives know. She's been trying to get you to the beach. Why don't you go?"

"The factory . . ."

Bill waved a hand as if to dismiss the factory. "Just because you're singlehandedly responsible for this factory's success as our New York representative . . ."

"Well, it *is* the best of its kind . . ."

". . . doesn't mean you have to kill yourself. Why, you should be enjoying the fruits of your labors."

"And just because a man's 61 doesn't mean he's ready for pasture!"

By June (it was 1929) Roger was forced to cut his working day because of his increasing dis-ease. Finally, he was ordered by his physician to stay in bed for two or three days until his blood could be examined. When Bill went to see him, he found Roger languishing uncharacteristically among the pillows with only a flicker of his usual good spirits. Beth worried about, hushing Bill with, "He has a fever. Please don't upset him."

Roger fretted, of course, about the factory. But the crisis he had feared came about, not in his business but in his health. In the heat of July he went back to work, with nearly fatal consequences . . .

On a particularly close day, he loosened his tie to allow any stray breeze to touch his moist neck. The office fan rotating overhead did little to help. The papers in front of him blurred. A brief vision of his wife and daughter relaxing by the ocean passed before his eyes. An unaccountable weak, dizzy feeling gripped him, and a strange blackness descended.

Roger regained consciousness in the Tannhurst Hospital, under the care of Dr. Fred Galagher, a leading physician. Several specialists examined him. X-rays by Dr. Kern, a prominent Atlanta doctor, showed that, according to his diagnosis, he had advanced tuberculosis.

Unaware of all this, Bill had decided to write Edgar Cayce about Roger's condition. Both men had previously sought information through the Virginia psychic on business and health matters. Bill had been the one, in fact, to introduce Roger to Cayce's work several years before. Bill's faith in Cayce stemmed from his own experience with the readings. From New York he now wrote: "I am writing this special request to ask you to get a check on these three questions for Mr. McDermott . . ." including his blood supply, fever, and cure. However, before Cayce received the letter, Bill received a call from Beth. "Roger's critically ill!" She said, "The doctors think there's no hope."

In response to a wire from Bill to Cayce, a reading was given on July 12. This was Roger's third, the last one having been given on April 1 for overactive kidneys due to poor eliminations. "Yes, we have the body, Roger McDermott," Cayce began now. "This we have had before.

"Now, we find the physical conditions are depleted with this body, as the result of strain, both mental and physical, and as affect the heart and blood supply of the body.

"The temperature as arises in system is produced by that of the bacilli as is carried in the blood stream from that of poor eliminations, combined with those of uric acid reaction, though not wholly a condition of the uric acid: this is aiding the condition in raising temperature, and the weakness or faintness from same." (2597-3)

(Roger was to write later: "We work nearly one thousand men and owing to the stress of my duties, I was in a very run down condition.")

The reading recommended eliminations being properly set up: "To bring the better results for the body, we would change somewhat the *surroundings* of the body. Through the activities of those properties as will aid in eliminations being properly set up, that do not over strain the functioning of the kidneys with the normalcy of the liver functioning, will tend to reduce the cause of conditions. These may be brought about through many channels, dependent upon which ones would be used. *We* would suggest those of the homeopathic remedies. Do that."

On the fifteenth, the fourth reading said that he would ultimately recover if no complications occurred. This reading said that the doctor had not diagnosed his case entirely correctly, although he was receiving the right treatment, so it should be kept.

Roger was given a blood transfusion, according to his doctor's treatment; and was told by Cayce that he should add iodine to his system, plus iron and calcium, by means of a device first described in earlier readings which he called the radio-active appliance. Eliminations were important, for the drosses of the blood could easily bring about recurrent bacilli. But the appliance treatment would not be possible yet.

On July 26 Roger was told by Cayce that he could leave the hospital when he was able to walk in the open air. He would recuperate best in Virginia Beach, where he could benefit from the radium in sand packs "which carry both the gold and the iodine . . . and for the appliances that may be attached to the body that would aid in alleviating these conditions as seen in the thyroids."[1]

With Roger on his way to Virginia Beach, Bill wrote: "Mr. McDermott, I believe, will arrive with his nurse Friday or Saturday. Mrs. McDermott will probably come along. . ." He asked that two connecting rooms be given

[1] It is difficult to think of the present headquarters building on 67th Street as a hospital: where once were hospital rooms and wards, there are now offices, apartments, and a library. The porches that surround the front and sides had been built with recuperation of patients in mind; once, indeed, patients had been wheeled out to catch the morning sun and the fresh salt breezes that wash up from the ocean. Now the porches are enjoyed by visitors and staff members to whom the days of the hospital are somehow unreal and remote, and the drama of sickness and recovery but a twice-told tale.

The Cayce Hospital had been dedicated November 11, 1928, and was under the supervision of Thomas B. House, M.D., of Hopkinsville, Kentucky, until his death in October, 1929. He was succeeded by Lyman A. Lydic, D.O., of Dayton, Ohio. Gena L. Crews, D.O., took over supervision of patients after the departure of Dr. Lydic. Other staff physicians were: Grace Berger, D.O.; Robert W. Woodhouse, M.D.; and James M. Parker, M.D.

By 1930 the hospital was accepting patients from New York State and North Carolina, as well as Tidewater. A few were out-patients, not actually occupying beds in the hospital. When the hospital closed in February, 1930, Edgar Cayce had appointments six months in advance.

The institution had everything in its favor: a staff sympathetic to and knowledgeable of the Cayce concepts of healing; a beautiful, wholesome setting beside the ocean; proximity to Washington and New York. With the economic upset of the time, however, support was withdrawn by its prime benefactors and it was never reactivated.

them for easy access to the sun porch on the second floor. He pointed out with some satisfaction that when Roger's associates and friends back home heard how much the readings were helping him, new friends would be won for the hospital.

Roger was admitted on August 8 by Dr. Berger, to be treated for Streptocosis. (2597-5) He was to stay, said his reading, for three to four weeks.

He continued to improve but was warned against overtaxing himself under stress because of his heart's inability to store energy as yet. Cayce further warned that he might become too dependent on digitalis and if assimilations were to fail, the result would be a heart block. As the amount of digitalis was decreased, to prevent his circulation becoming taxed, pellets were recommended containing sulphate of quinine, muriated iron, and rhubarb, one a day. This would help him rest better, along with frequent massage of his cerebro-spinal system—first with tepid water, then cold water, then equal parts of olive oil and tincture of myrrh.

He was to get out in the open air as much as possible but was to have no crowds of people in his room, especially in the evening. Roger was still a very sick man.

He was too weak to walk yet, and it would be ten days before he could go into the water. Even the sand packs would be too hard on his heart. He was to take blood-building foods, especially those carrying iron, and all fruits except apples and bananas. The juices of meats rather than fleshy portions were best.

On August 22 he was told he could "add days, months, years to his life . . . thus enabling the body to accomplish mentally and physically and spiritually much as has been desired. (2597-7)"

Roger again worried that the factory might not run without him. Edgar found him on the porch with Beth, scheming how he would travel to New York and to the factory in Tannhurst. He would see about his business, then return to the hospital, he pointed out.

"We'll ask about it in tomorrow's reading," Edgar said.

The reading of August 28 told him that such a trip would actually be good for him, he had improved so much, provided he didn't overtax himself. But the worries of his well-meaning family would *cause* him to be anxious. (2597-8)

Sure enough, Beth pleaded, "Please don't try to go back to your business too soon."

"I won't overdo, I promise."

Cayce, in the middle, reiterated that such warnings were unnecessary: "The body *won't* overtax itself."

"The body" didn't. Eventually, he took the sand packs and osteopathic treatments. Five weeks after arriving, he was released to return to New York to report to the president of his firm for duty.

In a report dated April 10, 1930, Roger wrote Edgar: "I have never felt better in my life than I have felt in the past eight months and I agree with Dr. S. who, in a letter to me, stated that I was out of the hands of the doctor and in the hands of God, and you no doubt have been the means for the information to come from God Himself to save my life and to you, again, I say, I owe my thanks. I certainly enjoyed the personal attention received from you, your doctors and nurses at the institution, and if at any time I can be of service to you or others, you have but to command . . ."

Some years later, Dr. S. wrote to Edgar Cayce: "At the request of Mrs. B. [an A.R.E. member] I am sending Mr. McDermott's medical statements to you at Virginia Beach. It is a real joy to see a man so useful, so big-hearted, so capable, and above all, a friend, snatched from death, as it were, and apparently restored to health. I frankly confess that it was little short of a miracle, as *practically 95% of such cases of streptococcic infection do not survive* [Author's italics]. We doctors do not take the credit; I feel that a Higher Power directed the case.

"I am naturally extremely interested in Mr. Cayce and his work. Some of these days I hope to run up to Virginia Beach to see him and the Hospital . . ."

Such records of testimony to treatment and cures through psychic means say a great deal about the Cayce Hospital—that it was justified and that it did not exist, however briefly, in vain.

You could have asked Roger McDermott.

Medical Commentary: Streptococcus

by William A. McGarey

In 1928, the medical profession had little therapy for a streptococcus septicemia, which this case apparently turned out to be, despite an earlier diagnosis by x-ray of advanced tuberculosis. Today, therapy would have been given earlier, and undoubtedly adequately, in the form of antibiotics. It is interesting that Sir Arthur Fleming discovered penicillin at about the same time these readings were given, although it took fifteen years before clinical application of the discovery actually came about to any degree. But in 1928 and 1929, a strep infection was, indeed, a fearful thing.

The fact that the attending physician saw this 61-year-old man's recovery as such an unlikely event and attended by influences from a "Higher Power" still is not perhaps the most remarkable thing about this particular case. Cayce, while giving his first reading on this illness, stated himself that correction could be "brought about through many channels, dependent upon which ones would be used.

We would suggest those of the homeopathic remedies." Cayce apparently saw that the doctors would probably not use homeopathy, although he saw that as being preferable in this case.

Actually, a blood transfusion—among other things—was one of the principal therapies in the acute stages. Cayce stated that there should be no fear of the outcome and recommended that the care and treatment being given at the time should be followed, as it was of course. McDermott was able to transfer from Tannhurst Hospital to the Cayce Hospital in Virginia Beach.

Perhaps the most remarkable thing about this story is the host of questions and implications that arise from a serious study of the events as they took place in the course of this man's illness. More questions than answers, certainly; and more implications than evidence. Can a "sleeping" individual, for instance, foresee the outcome of a disease with accuracy, sufficiently to set at rest the worries of concerned family? What is the nature of a disease process? Is it found in the bacteria that enter the body in some manner; or does the body itself, through stresses and lack of balance within—created through improper use of life activities—bring about the disease condition, opening the way for bacteria to finish the job of complete disruption?

Let's trace the history of the septicemia and examine the explanation of things from Cayce's point of view, asking the questions and dealing with the implications as we go along. The human body, certainly, is one of the most fascinating subjects anyone can study, and we certainly know little about it at the present time. About its structure, maybe yes; but about its workings, its activities, the forces, the energies, the relationships, the coordinating activities, the coordinating intelligence—in other words, the function of the body—definitely no.

Cayce's very first reading for this man, given fifteen months before his severe illness began, pointed up a lack of coordination in the eliminating systems of the body which had established a chronicity that was apparently not fully corrected even though Cayce suggested at that point a manner in which it might be returned to normal. The kidneys apparently were not eliminating from the body the substances which they should due to their overstimulation from the very nature of the stresses this man was placing on himself in his work. This buildup of what Cayce often called "drosses" had to be eliminated in some manner, and the liver, the capillaries and lymphatics of the intestinal tract suffered as a result. This congestion then brought about a focal point of malfunction which Cayce called a "lesion," which in turn produced certain symptoms. He told his story like this:

. . . There is seen that for some time back there has been the tendency towards the non-eliminations in the proper channel, and with the constant effect of an over-stimulation to the kidneys has brought that of the uremic forces to be active in an improper manner. Not that this is as uremia, or uremic poisoning, but an overactive kidney gives to the whole system the improper distribution of eliminating forces in body to the excess of the liver and to the excess of capillary or lymphatic circulation, and eliminations. Hence we have the character of hindrance through congestion in the intestinal tract, and a form of lesion as produces stitch in side. Pressure produced on nerves of the limbs brings tautness and inactivity through the nerves *of* the limbs. Then the condition becoming acute, these are brought about in an acute form.

Cayce suggested at this point that McDermott take a three-day course of therapy that has similarities to treatments used thousands of years ago. A pint of sage tea and a pint of saffron tea, taken as hot as possible each day, followed by a steam bath to sweat the teas "through the body." Then, after a three-day rest, a series of osteopathic treatments. The sweats, Cayce said, would start proper eliminations through the alimentary canal, while

51

the osteopathy would set up the proper coordination in the nervous system.

Both these herbs have anti-spasmodic activities. In addition, saffron (*Crocus sativus*) is a stimulant, gives tone to the stomach, and is used to promote the secretion of sweat and of urine. The sage (*Salvia officinalis*) tea, on the other hand, has been used in times past for nervous conditions, coughs and colds, and any condition where a sweat is desired. It also produces perspiration. Both are classed, therefore, among herbs as diaphoretics.

There is record made that McDermott took the teas but no evidence that he ever followed with the sweats or the osteopathic treatments. He did improve with the teas, recovering from a 24-hour syndrome which was progressively diagnosed as a stroke, then as blood poisoning, then as the gout. He was not hospitalized for this problem, but recovered rather promptly.

Then, working hard and encouraging what many call a severe stress syndrome, this man fell apart physically. Cayce stated that it was the strain rather than the infection which caused the heart and the circulation to be in such serious condition. The septicemia, he implied, came about because of poor elimination of an acute nature (probably affecting both the liver and the kidneys) added to a chronic imbalance in the organs of elimination, probably dating back to the inadequate therapy of more than a year previous. This imbalance, Cayce maintained, resulted in an increase in the blood uric acid and contributed in a large degree to the febrile condition of the body. Cayce agreed certainly with the anatomic and physiologic description of elimination in the body as coming about through the lymphatic system, the liver and intestines, the kidneys, the lungs, and the skin.

In the Cayce view of physiology, it can readily be seen why therapy of the first magnitude was to be elimination of the drosses in the system. Properly achieved, eliminations would protect the kidneys from serious damage and aid in restoring more of a normal function in the liver.

Gradually, then, a balanced eliminatory system would be achieved which would "reduce the cause of conditions." This was where Cayce suggested homeopathy as his choice of therapy.

Assimilation apparently had become a serious problem here also. The ineffectiveness of the process of taking into the body the food which is needed and changing it sufficiently so that its energies may be utilized in all parts of the body in restoration and regeneration of body tissues —this ineffectiveness had brought about certain glandular changes, particularly in the thyroid, which in turn disturbed the distribution of these energies or forces into their proper channels. A complicated picture, to be sure.

A diet was important to the body, a diet designed so that it would not add to the wastes which needed to be eliminated . . . but which would help in keeping a balance.

The recuperating patient was then told, on the fourteenth day of his illness, that he would need three or four weeks of rest, preferably at Virginia Beach. There he could get "more of the applications as to meet the needs of conditions for the physical body."

These "applications" provide for us perhaps the most interesting part of the entire reading, not for what they *are* as much as for what they imply. Cayce suggested in one sentence that McDermott could take sand packs at Virginia Beach and receive beneficial vibrations to the functioning of his body from the radium, gold, and iodine found in the sand; and that by using what Cayce called a radio-active appliance, he could receive further benefits in a vibrational manner from iodine, calcium, and iron. These would aid the thyroid in its function and further balance and assist the assimilation of the body.

If Cayce was correct in what he talked about while asleep, we do indeed know little about the inner, secret workings of the human body!

A sand pack is a simple thing, certainly—one must allow himself to be covered and packed with sand up to his neck. Cayce said the Virginia Beach sand was unique in its content of gold in the amounts which would be therapeutic. He advised against McDermott doing this too soon, before his recovery had gained to a certain point, for it might be a distress rather than an aid. But we seldom think of radium, gold, and iodine coming from such a pleasant interlude on the beach, at least as a therapeutic modality.

The radio-active appliance was described in many of the Cayce readings as being beneficial in a variety of ailments of the human body. Its value was seen as being, again, vibrational. A small cylindrical item when put together according to Cayce's specifications, it stands about six inches high and is two inches in diameter. It has two leads, like an ordinary battery, although it is not a battery; and plates from the two wire leads are attached to the body in a specified manner. In this particular reading, as in many others, Cayce implied that one of the wires should pass through a solution jar which would have in it a solution containing iron, calcium, and iodine.

The vibration of these elements, then, would be carried into the body through the wire by a flow of energy which Cayce stated was inherent in every living human being, and which, apparently, activated the appliance without external electrical energy being introduced. Engineers have puzzled over this device, and some testing has been done. But no definitive answers have really been arrived at.

The appliance, as described in many of Cayce's readings, is basically two five-inch bars of carbon steel drilled and tapped for copper wire leads at the top, a half-inch wide and a quarter-inch thick, separated by two one-eighth-inch-thick sections of glass the same length and width. These are surrounded completely by bars of carbon on all four sides, and the assembly is set in crushed hardwood charcoal inside a regular 16-ounce tin can, which is then sealed over the top. Small copper plates at the end of the wires are used to be applied to the body when the appliance is in operation. And Cayce insisted that the appliance be set in ice water when used. There is no known means of generating energy in this way at the present time, but Cayce saw this as a means of gentle, yet real therapy to the body.

Fascinating questions arise. And there are partial answers available. Is there a flow of energy in the human body which we have not yet discovered? Is there an energy field around the body? Is this what has been called the aura? Cayce described such a flow of energy, in the form of a figure-eight, crossing at the area of the solar plexus. He also described the aura of the human being as being a type of force field, visible only to those who can "see" it, but present in all individuals. Shafica Karagulla (*Breakthrough to Creativity*) told how the psychics she worked with saw the same figure-eight flow of energy, the same aura. Eemans described the same thing and reported a wealth of experiments using copper screens under the body and wires to bring about a therapeutic result. Similar reports and practices have been repeated down through the ages, from the time of ancient Egypt.

The ancient practice of acupuncture is based on the principle that there are specific points in the body where such a flow of energy is specifically contacted by inserting special needles. In recent years, using Kirlian photography, Russian scientists have photographed energies spurting out of these specific areas. They have also photographed the aura. In their minds, little doubt exists that these forces created by the human body are real and active. They are, in fact, observable and recordable in all living things.

As McDermott's recuperation continued, Cayce at one point foresaw an impending heart block plus a possible assimilatory failure of one type or another, due to the dependence of the body on the stimulation given the heart by the digitalis. He suggested in its place a small dosage of quinine sulfate, muriated iron, and rhubarb, to be phased in as the digitalis was phased out. We, of course, have no way of determining whether this man might in reality have developed a heart block. As his activities were gradually increased, however, as he obtained osteopathic treatments, special massages, the sand packs, a special diet, the treatments with the radio-active appliance, he recovered in fine style, following fully the suggestions Cayce gave while in a psychic state—what we now call an extended state of consciousness.

This case provokes a great number of questions which I shall pose, but not even attempt to answer. They constitute, in my mind, a challenge to the open-mindedness of the medical and scientific community, and to the government agencies which might encourage and support research into the nature of this wonderful thing that allows us to express ourselves in this three-dimensional consciousness—the human body. These questions all need reasonable answers:

1. Has diet been underestimated in its physiological effect on the human body?
2. Do herbs as used throughout the ages have a therapeutic effect that is measureable? And is the effect principally one to change the coordination of the body forces, perhaps? Or to aid an organ in its function?
3. Does elimination as a total body function really play this large role in the health of the body that Cayce suggests?
4. Is assimilation a recognizable entity in the body? Does it become an all-or-none phenomenon, or is it a force with a multitude of tasks, any one of which might become weakened or deficient?
5. Does physical therapy act only on the muscular structures of the body or does it perform a therapeutic duty to the uncoordinated functional organism?
6. Does osteopathy alter the physiological function of a human body in a therapeutic manner?
7. How does vibration work in relation to body functions?

8. Does a sand pack do more than introduce a tranquilizing effect into the body? What about related treatments from health spas around the world: mud packs, hot mineral baths, steam baths, uranium mine sitting, copper bracelets?
9. Does gold play a part in the normal function of the body?
10. Can the "vibration" of an element be carried into the energy field of a person so that the function of glands of the body is enhanced?
11. Can the flow of energy in the body itself activate an appliance which has no source of energy within itself?

How mankind may be healed is a subject which has stretched the imagination and ingenuity of men throughout the ages. It has not stopped today simply because we have achieved a degree of scientific accomplishment in the physical sciences. Cayce's suggestions given to a man with a serious disease offer to us more of that stretching of the mind. This, I think, is good.

A Mother's Ordeal

by Mary Ellen Carter

Five-year-old Suzy Paxton lifted the spoon to her mouth, but before she could take the morsel of oatmeal, her hand twisted and the spoon clattered to the table. Helen, her mother, watched with mild surprise. "You haven't forgotten how to feed yourself, have you?"

Again the child attempted to lift the spoon to her mouth, but it jammed an eye, instead. In an angry little storm of frustration she picked up the bowl and threw it to the floor, splattering the contents and broken pieces. "Dumb old bowl!"

Patiently, Helen picked up the pieces and cleaned the linoleum. When the incident had been repeated, she resignedly fed Suzy, herself.

Soon afterward, Suzy was trying to draw her letters when her face suddenly twitched contortedly. The strange quirk became a habit. Puzzled, Helen tried to admonish her daughter. The time-honored command "Don't do that!" only served to frustrate Suzy further.

Now, she was increasingly unable to do the simple tasks she had learned readily. Her coordination was so bad that Helen was forced to do many chores for her, including dressing and undressing her. Suzy's temper tantrums became more frequent.

When she started to school, Suzy seemed to benefit from the change and the challenge. She had already learned her letters; numbers were no special problem. She was a good student, said her teacher. Until, that is, one day when the teacher, Miss Dresden, called to say, "I'm sorry, but Suzy has been very impudent these past few weeks. At first, I corrected her mildly. Now, she's worse. She has become disruptive and disobedient."

"What! . . . in what way?" Helen asked, her heart sinking.

"She called me 'an old cow,' and said she wasn't coming in when recess was over. I had to make her stay in the cloak room. She threw quite a tantrum."

"I am sorry. I'll try to talk to her."

Suzy's personality didn't improve. At home, at play with other children, she became a handful. One day, as she and Katey played with their dolls in the dining room, Suzy tore the head off Katey's beloved doll, then danced around the room in a frenzy. Her movements, Helen noted as she came in answer to Katey's cry, were a series of jerky steps.

"Don't cry, Katey," soothed Helen, as she picked up Wanda's head and cottony body, "we'll sew her back together, good as new."

The doll was easy to deal with. Suzy was not.

In the years that followed, Suzy was taken to doctors for help. However, there seemed to be no one in the medical profession who could help her. Certainly, teachers and principals were at a loss as to how to handle the girl. Her condition worsened, even as she grew into her teens. At fifteen, she tried hard to seem normal, as though she

59

realized that her problem was alienating her from her peers. A boy might come courting, but at her compulsive rudeness and jerky antics, he was soon discouraged.

One young man who came to the house tried to laugh off her strange ways. "Give me a chance," he said.

Billy did all the talking. He talked mostly about basketball, and Suzy seemed glad to be with him. But then she made a cutting remark and bolted into the house. Helen happened to be in the yard, raking leaves. She saw Billy's surprised expression and his frown.

He glanced at her, puzzled. "Mrs. Paxton," he asked, "what's wrong with Suzy?"

There was no answer. To all who asked the same question, Helen had no words. Her husband's people became quite critical of *her*, and she recalls even now the remarks they made. "Poor discipline," she was told.

"I know how *I* would handle that imp!" said another.

Helen began to avoid them. She kept her feelings to herself. She felt that even her husband didn't understand her frustration at coping with their child. They had other children, all normal and well-adjusted. Suzy remained an enigma.

When Helen once more confronted the child with her poor report card (she neglected her books, apt though she was), she pointed out her truancy record as well.

Suzy flew into a rage. She stomped the floor, yelling, "Stop nagging me!"

By the time she was seventeen, in her third year at high school, the authorities there despaired. Her intolerable behavior marked by frequent outbursts in the classroom led to her dismissal. At home, Helen found her daughter increasingly irritable and helpless. She was obliged to bathe and feed her and to try to control her tantrums. When guests came to the house, the family was often embarrassed by the girl's unsociable behavior.

Physicians termed her condition a nervous disorder but

could find little effective treatment for her; chiropractic was tried with no results.

Helen grew frantic. The burden of coping with her daughter all these years tested her endurance. To her horror, she found herself considering suicide. Peering into the gas oven one day, she thought that she might end her misery very easily—or else herself be committed to an asylum.

* * *

"I first heard of Edgar Cayce when I had trouble with my daughter," Helen told me. She spoke softly as she recalled her traumatic experience. The years had brought serenity to her fine features. She sat in the living room of another daughter in Chesapeake, Virginia. It was 1969, nearly 40 years later. A slender, greying woman, she has lived with this daughter and son-in-law since her husband died in 1968.

She spoke of her memories of Gertrude and Edgar Cayce and their influence on her and her family. "I was talking one day across my porch railing to a neighbor, Mrs. Bartlett. We were telling each other our troubles, particularly those concerning our children. I had only recently heard of Edgar Cayce. She didn't think much of him.

"He was giving lectures at Virginia Beach. Mrs. Bartlett telephoned down there and learned there was to be a lecture by a Mr. Morton Blumenthal."

They went to the lecture. "It was *Tertium Organum*. It was all so far above my head. I don't remember much except that he talked about the fourth dimension and its relationship to Mr. Cayce's ability."

After the lecture, Helen told her friend, "This is what I've been looking for all my life."

"But I thought you couldn't understand the lecture."

"I understand a lot with my heart."

Even then, Helen was slow to get help from Edgar Cayce. She obtained a reading, however, for a friend's baby suffering from a spastic condition causing brain damage.

The Cayce Hospital had just opened its doors. Although many of her friends and acquaintances in Norfolk scoffed at the Cayce work, Helen persisted in learning more about it. She decided to have a reading for Suzy, who was now 20.

Suzy's first reading was given January 24, 1930. Helen was present with her, in addition to Gertrude, Edgar, Gladys Davis, a friend of Helen's (name withheld), and Dr. W. H. McChesney.*

Suzy's trouble, Helen told me, had started with diphtheria at the age of four. According to her reading at 20, the diphtheria antitoxin serum which was given to her had destroyed her assimilation. Her system could no longer take the amount of iodine necessary for balance. The thyroid was trying to provide a balance in the nerves, but it could not.

"There are deficiencies in the supply of nutriment through some of the channels," stated the reading, "and these, corrected, would bring better responses . . . These conditions have to do with the glands and the supply to the organs . . . Not that the body is not normal, save in this respect."

She needed iodine in her blood; she had an excess of potassium. There was an overactivity in her nerve system "and unless changes are brought about, the thyroids must suffer eventually . . . or there must be the reaction of same in the mental deficiency of the body . . ."

Her mental forces "as related to command, demand, and duty suffer from the loss of balance due to this deficiency." Her internal organs were normal.

She needed application of vibrations—low electrical— "that will cause the building up of the deficiencies and equalizing them through food values."

There was no mental unbalance but there was a lack of thyroid secretion to keep her equilibrium: ". . . not

* His real name.

62

mental deficiency, no. Coordinating deficiency." Treatment would best be conducted in the Cayce Hospital. She would recover completely if the readings were fully carried out, and it would take only six to nine weeks.

Her next reading, given after her admittance, instructed the use of the wet cell battery charged with iodine. The copper plate was to be applied first to her wrist and the larger, nickel plate or anode at the umbilicus. At first, it was not to be applied for longer than thirty minutes at a time.

The instructions were carried out. According to further readings, the copper anode was placed at the base of her brain, or at the first and second cervical; the larger anode, at the ninth dorsal. Now the battery was applied for sixty minutes twice a day. Manipulations were given daily for her entire system, and corrections were given osteopathically. Her diet included quantities of shell fish, but no clams. She was to have no hog meat or bread. At least twice a week, she was given codliver oil and calves' liver. After two weeks, a reading said that she should have more body-, blood- and nerve-building material in her food, but not before changes had taken place in the glands through use of the battery. She needed more iodine. By March 3, suppressions causing her incoordination had been alleviated, said her reading. Particular attention should be given now to a local condition in the pelvic organs. Eliminations were to be corrected by osteopathy. This method was to be used for coordinations to the brain center—the pineal and adrenal—to be stimulated. The staff was to help Suzy in learning to coordinate her mental and physical bodies by guiding and controlling her reading, studying, and general activities. She was to have definite tasks to perform. Her reading explained that it was important that staff members make sure *their* activities and thoughts were in keeping with their attempt to bring about healing!

By March 24, said a reading, more improvements had occurred during the past week than had occurred up to then. There was relief in the pressure in the lumbar or pelvic regions. Coordinations had been effected through the ninth and tenth dorsal region. The treatments were to continue.

As Suzy improved, Helen had time to collect her thoughts and to wonder what had brought about this painful relationship between herself and her daughter. She decided that a life reading would clarify matters. So in the next reading for Suzy, Helen asked at the end, "Would a life reading be a help?"

"Not at present," was the answer. "It's the physical forces that we must combat at the present." It explained that Suzy's condition was accentuated by influences in her past experience and also by the influence of the moon . . .

"This would be very interesting to the physician in charge—to watch the changes in the moon and watch the effect it has upon the body," was the volunteered comment. It added that following the new moon, she would exhibit "a wild, hilarious reaction." As the moon waned, her condition would become better. These, however, were merely influences which might be overcome by treatment in progress.

Here Cayce introduced for the first time the idea that the book of Revelation was related to the functions of the human body. It would be very good, he suggested, for the doctor attending Suzy to read it and understand it! "Especially in reference to this body." (2501-6) Just why this was so was not elaborated upon.

Less pressure on Suzy's solar plexus center had been brought about so that there was less incoordination through the pineal gland from the effects of the sympathetic system. The attitudes of the hospital staff were again pointed out as being particularly effective. They would help her even more if their attitudes were more positive, both physically and mentally.

Now that the pelvic and lumbar regions were more nearly aligned, said Cayce in the mid-April reading, principal emphasis should be given those centers where the cerebro-spinal and sympathetic were coordinant with the physical forces. Areas concerned were the third and fourth cervical, the second and third dorsal, the ninth and tenth dorsal plexus, and the fourth lumbar. Following stimulating (not deep) manipulations osteopathically, low electrical vibrations should be applied.

Again, Suzy's mental and spiritual environment should be planned for her welfare: "Well that due consideration be given to the environment of the mental activities—that is, as to *what* is read, *what* is said, to *whom,* and *where.* These not as suppressions, these not as hindrances. Rather as guiding and as counselling with that being created in the mental activities of the body."

In this reading, Helen asked for an explanation of the reference to The Revelation in connection with the patient. The Revelation, Cayce replied, contains the illustration of how the mental body is raised in consciousness to the "holy mount," such activity taking place through the glandular functions of the body. When Suzy was taken home, the best environment for her would be not that of any particular sect or "ism," but where the activities of individuals were sincere in their efforts. Where, she now asked, could the doctor study The Revelation in this new light?

". . . *any*one," said Cayce, "will they study that given in the Book and compare same to the anatomical conditions of a physical body, will learn the *spiritual* body, the *mental* body—not metaphysics, either!"

Study was undertaken by various persons of this subject, and today there are books and tapes available on The Revelation and the seven spiritual centers.

Helen had been sorely tried by her conflicts with her daughter for the past sixteen years. Suzy had developed toward her an attitude of rebellion. In return Helen had at times displayed the opposite of loving indifference, however much she attempted to control herself. Now, she wanted to begin again to reach her daughter and heal the breach. In asking how to begin, she was told that the young woman's physical healing must be accomplished first, and "both must, then, change" that there be no longer mere tolerance, "but a loving affection between each, that is not even akin to tolerance!"

After dismissal from the hospital, Suzy continued to improve; and, in a year's time, she was married. She had three children, all of whom are grown, married, and with families of their own. At 60, she has seven grandchildren and one great grand-child.

And that makes Helen a very happy great, great grand-mother!

Medical Commentary: Incoordination

by William A. McGarey, M.D.

Incoordination and neurasthenia are two of the labels listed in the indexing system of the Cayce readings to describe the condition under which Helen's little daughter, Suzy, lived for over fifteen years of her life. We have no diagnoses in the medical literature to identify her specific condition today—if Cayce's clairvoyance was accurate—for incoordination of these nervous systems of ours is not at the present time a disease entity. It should be, for function is as real as is an organ of the body. And units of the body must function in coordination with other units or, obviously, an incoordination is present.

Incoordination of the voluntary muscular movement is described in medical dictionaries as an inability to bring into common, harmonious movement or action. But the other kind of incoordination is perhaps a new thought, although obviously, if it exists at all, it has had a part in the illnesses of mankind since mankind first appeared on the earth.

Neurasthenia, on the other hand, is an inaccurate diagnosis or description of Suzy's illness. The weaknesses, generalized fatigability, lack of energy, and general avoidance of activity of any kind found in true neurasthenia gives the condition its name, of course. But these are not the symptoms found in the little girl when she became ill, nor in the developing child and teen-ager as she found many difficulties in life.

Today, perhaps the best diagnosis we could offer for such a condition is that of the hyperactive child. This is still a name which is descriptive only of a clinical condition and which covers undoubtedly a multitude of underlying causative factors and apparent objective findings.

If such a child were brought into most doctors' offices, however, she would be termed a hyperactive child and be treated as such.

In a recent communication, Pecci describes some twenty factors as causative in the condition of so-called hyperactivity. Whether these are factual or not, there is no question but that the hyperactive syndrome finds its origins in many diverse causative factors. How the hyperactivity is produced in the living body of the individual, however, has never been fully understood, nor is it clear how some drugs have given an apparent beneficial effect.

Cayce's description of the illness present in this child is fascinating to follow for a number of reasons. First, it comes from a psychic source; second, it describes functions of the physiological organism as they bring about a diseased state; third, it pins down an antitoxin as the primary cause; fourth, it poses the possibility that there is an endocrine factor present in this case and probably other similar conditions; fifth, it suggests that there can be active in any human body a very real emotional change brought about by the phases of the moon; sixth, it states that the book of the Revelation in the New Testament deals with the function of the human body; and seventh, it implies that this factor of incoordination of the nervous systems could be etiologic in most of the conditions that we presently call hyperactivity.

At the age of four, Suzy contracted diphtheria. She was given antitoxin serum as part of her treatment, a standard and effective therapy of that day which dated back to the late 1890's in its use. In 1914, the antiserum had more than twenty years of experience behind it, so was at that point a well developed therapeutic tool which had proved its effectiveness. Suzy, so ill that she required an airway in order to breathe, was given a series of injections of the antitoxin before she finally pulled through. It was after this episode that the young girl's symptoms began.

It is interesting that Cayce related the entire syndrome of 16 years' duration to the administration of the diphtheria antitoxin. He did not attribute symptoms or deficient physiological conditions to the diphtheria itself but saw the deficiency of iodine and the excess of potassium as coming directly from the antitoxin.

The development of the full clinical condition as Cayce seemed to reconstruct the event is not a biochemically-oriented etiologic process, but rather a sequential story of happenings which undoubtedly are associated with a variety of functions and chemical reactions.

First, Cayce implied that the antitoxin caused the body to be unable to assimilate iodine properly. Whatever the disruption that brought this about, it created at the same time an excess of potassium in the blood stream. The thyroid glands suffered from the lack of iodine in what must be considered to be a rather unique manner. Cayce saw that the lack of proper thyroid hormone secreted into the blood brought in turn an over-activity of certain nerve centers in the autonomic nervous system, especially as they related to the functioning of some of the organs of the body and—

as is seen in the activities of the mental forces as related to command, demand, and duty—and in this respect, the loss of the effect of the balance is that which brings the effect of this deficiency in the system. (2501-1)

What this means in the final stabilized condition of the human body is that an incoordination was created between the cerebrospinal nervous system and the autonomic. In this case, Suzy's mother had then a major problem of child care on her hands: a severe case of hyperkinesis, maladaption, or whatever one might wish to call it. Cayce called it simply an incoordination which could be corrected with proper care.

As therapy was begun almost immediately after the first reading given for this twenty-year-old young lady, changes began inside the body; and they were carefully documented in subsequent psychic comments as further directions were given. I, at least, get a real thrill and sense of wonder when in the course of events in a story such as this something completely unexpected shows up in a simple, off-hand manner—an idea that leads one to a field of interest and study that seemingly has no end.

An example: does a book in the Bible have a place in the classroom of medical schools, demonstrating how subtle forces of the body play a part in health and disease? I would probably receive few affirmative answers to such a question from physiology professors, but Cayce would have this come about. In Suzy's sixth reading, he pointed out that there were pressures existing in the lumbar and sacral regions of the body which activated a force which, in Eastern religions, is called the kundalini energy. These forces rise up to and through the pineal gland,

which corresponds to those forces as are spoken of, even in that of the Book of The Revelation. Be very good for the doctor here to read The Revelation and understand it! Especially in reference to this body! These forces as applied to this are the activities as are seen in the sympathetic nerve system, and *advance* in their activities as the force of same impel through the sympathetic and the cerebrospinal plexus from the 9th dorsal to the brain itself. (2501-6)

70

The Revelation, as a means of understanding the creative forces within the body and as a kind of textbook of endocrinologic study, was thus mentioned for the first time in the readings. A question was asked about this in the next readings, in which Cayce indicated that an illustration is given in the Revelation showing how the "mental body" is raised through various degrees of consciousness. The activity of this energy rises from the lower parts of the body through the correlated centers of an anatomical body, as consciousness in the autonomic nervous system is elevated "to the inner court, or in the holy mount, through the pineal gland—that coordinates with the sympathetic forces."

In answering a final question about how the doctor on the case could study the Revelation to obtain this information, Cayce briefly pointed out that "*anyone,* will they study that given in the Book and compare same to the anatomical conditions of a physical body, will *learn* the *spiritual* body, the *mental* body—*not* metaphysics either!" A fascinating statement which, if factual, might augment the projected study of the human body in the classrooms of our medical schools.

Astrology was still another area of subject material almost casually opened up to the interested reader in Suzy's sixth reading. Cayce's comments easily skipped over barriers and exceeded boundaries that man has carefully built up over the ages. The astrologer finds evidence that the moon, the closest of the other heavenly bodies, as well as the sun and the stars exert a material influence on the human being, his destiny and his very physical body. Medicine as a whole, however, finds lunar effects and the care of sick persons to be a combination not really compatible.

Cayce was not hampered, apparently, by prejudice toward any field of endeavor within the scope of man's interest and scientific study. He might comment easily—as he did here—that the moon and medicine are related, and almost let it go at that. But he didn't quite relinquish the idea. In describing how the doctor should use an electrically driven vibrator with a sponge applicator alongside the spinal column, he suggested that this quick vibratory motion would be especially effective with the double chain of sympathetic ganglia that lies deep in that area, and with the autonomic nervous system. The imbalance of the latter had "much to do with . . . the lunar conditions," or the emotional reactions to the waxing moon. Indeed, in Cayce's viewpoint, the body was an exceedingly intricate creation, sensitive to many influences, and capable of more than we presently suspect.

He was suggesting, apparently, that the manner in which the sympathetic-parasympathetic nervous system was unbalanced in its function and in its relationship to the rest of the nervous system was the primary reason for the moon to possibly have such an unusual effect on this person's emotions. The emotions are, after all, directly related to the unconscious portions of a person's makeup. They deal almost exclusively with the autonomic nervous system and the glandular functions of the body, at times seeming to be completely apart from any conscious (cerebrospinal) control.

This may be why Cayce suggested to the physician that it would be an instructive and interesting experience to observe and document Suzy's reactions to the phases of the moon. Had he been asked the question, it is quite likely that Mr. Cayce would also have suggested this as another course of study to be added to the medical schools' curricula.

The therapeutic program which Cayce outlined for this strange disorder of the body had several component parts. As a whole, however, it would seem best to call it a rehabilitation process, for it involved a number of therapeutic efforts. Osteopathy, physical therapy, low voltage electrotherapy, nutritional therapy, psychotherapy, a type of occupational therapy—all these were suggested. In addition, and perhaps overriding the entire therapeutic program, was the reaffirmed need for a physical-mental-spiritual coordination in treatment of the individual.

The staff of the hospital was instructed that their attitudes contributed in a very significant way to the healing process. The patient was informed—if she were to understand—that her acceptance of the various therapeutic modalities, her "response" to treatment, was a strong factor in the time-lapse during which healing might occur. In other words, if she responded in the most positive, creative, and constructive manner, her return to normal physical condition would be rapid. As events progressed, it appeared that she did not respond quite as expected, and the projected six to nine weeks that Cayce initially suggested lengthened out to six months. Why? "The manner in which the body responds to the applications that have been made." This was the answer Cayce gave to the question.

As advice was given toward the rehabilitation of these physiologic processes, the doctors attending the patient were not left out of the picture. The osteopaths were told in what manner the treatments were to be administered, what spinal areas were to be paid special attention. In Suzy's case, it was the second and third cervical, the second and third dorsal, the eighth and ninth dorsal, and the fourth lumbar. The study of the girl's reactions to the phases of the moon, the attention to be paid to the Revelation and its relationship to this person's abnormality —these, too, became part of the therapy.

The only medication suggested for Suzy was iodine, which had to be administered in a vibratory manner through the mechanism of a battery. This was constructed in a special way, and according to a voluminous group of Cayce's readings, designed to create a low voltage flow of electricity which would be introduced into the body. As stated in the readings, this device would then bring into the body the iodine which Cayce maintained could not pass the assimilatory barrier of the body as food was regularly taken into the body—at least not in sufficient amounts to make for the health of the body.

The fact that these various suggestions, when followed,

corrected the problem that was threatening to distort Suzy's entire life overshadows the knowledge that we do not know how such a battery could work or how essential a part it played in the curative process. But, then, we do not really know why one sperm cell out of thousands teeming around an ovum becomes the one which penetrates the cell-wall barrier and starts the process that eventually produces an individual. Whereas familiarity may not really breed contempt, certainly frequency breeds blind acceptance. We must be thankful for those who do ask the questions and work to find out the answers.

There were really two primary goals sought in Suzy's therapeutic program: one was the introduction of iodine into the system in such a manner that it could be used to aid the thyroid in its function; the second was the re-establishment of a coordination and a balance in the nervous systems of the body—the repair of an "incoordination" of functions within the human body. Thus we have a deficiency disease and a resulting functional, physiological incoordination which is a disease entity in itself and which can produce other problems in the body as well.

In approaching such a problem, Cayce apparently utilized a balanced program which took into consideration all aspects of the human being, assuming that all parts of a person are contributory to health and well-being. He suggested a course of therapy which is best described as physiological rehabilitation, correcting the processes of the body rather than healing the organs. In this case, the organic condition of the body was good; only the functions were aberrant.

That Suzy recovered well is pointed out adequately in her story. It is an interesting fact that we have a reading for this woman some twelve years after she left the Cayce Hospital, when she had found her place in the world as a wife and as a mother. It points out the emphasis usually found in the readings when dealing with the physical body and provides us with an end to our story:

Mr. Cayce: Yes, we have the body here—this we have had before, you see.

There are a great many changes that have taken place in the body since last we had same here. Most of these have been in the fulfilling or developing of the body and its activities, and in much bettered conditions in coordinating activities through the physical forces. (2501-12)

The Turning Point

by Mary Ellen Carter

Lila Haynes sat in the chair facing Dr. Merrill Dawson. She gripped her purse in her gloved hands and said, "Doctor, I'm a doctor, too—an osteopath. Tell me plainly what chances my boy has of coming through this?"

Dr. Dawson, large and kindly, shook his head. "I'm sorry, but all four of us physicians here have agreed his chances are very slight."

In her heart, Lila knew that this was the worst moment in her fifty-four years, and she did not trust herself to speak.

"A ruptured appendix is a dangerous thing to begin with," the man went on. "When he was operated on, his condition turned into peritonitis. There's even gangrene, now, I'm afraid. And he's contracted typhoid fever."

She stood up. "I must see him, please, if I may."

"Of course. You must realize he's very low. Only for a moment."

Phil Haynes, 28, lay drowsing under the sheet, only

partly aware that his mother had entered the room. He was limp and still, and a pallor lay on his features, as though death had already drawn a veil over them. He was thin from the ordeal of his illness.

Phil, himself, was an osteopath.

As she stood gazing down at her son, she prayed, "Oh, dear God, tell me what to do. Dear Great Physician, help me to help this young man who has dedicated his life to healing others. Surely You have a plan for him, and surely You don't mean for him to die!"

She heard light steps advancing down the hall. They were those of her daughter-in-law, Vivian, who had gone to telephone her parents about Phil's crisis. Vivian appeared in the room, her face wan with the strain. Lila told her, "Dear, stay with him while I go to make a phone call of my own."

The young woman nodded and looked with frightened eyes at her husband, who had been only a while ago so full of life and hopes for the future. She touched his hand. Lila went out, saying, "Don't give up hope yet." Vivian's head was bent, but at those words her heart seemed to lift.

For Lila had remembered that only a few months ago she had had a reading from Edgar Cayce—a "life" reading telling her of her former incarnations. She had heard of his ability to diagnose physical ailments, however, and had learned something of his success in giving helpful suggestions for healing. As an osteopath, she knew of the power the body has to heal itself when manipulated and aligned properly, and she knew that Edgar Cayce had recommended her particular healing art to a large number of people. All that she had seen and learned of his ability and treatments had been acceptable to her. She had thought, upon recognizing his work as a valid step toward progress in healing, that if ever she herself or a loved one were in need of his help, that she would not hesitate to seek it.

Now, there was no time to lose. She passed by the

elevator doors and went briskly down the stairs to the lobby to find a telephone. At this hour—6:15 in the evening—Mr. Cayce would doubtless be having dinner with his family. She hoped he would forgive her for the intrusion.

It had been a beautiful spring day at Virginia Beach. The Cayces had not yet sat down to eat dinner when the telephone rang. Edgar himself answered the ring. "Long distance," he told Gertrude, and waited.

A woman's soft voice began, "This is Lila Haynes. I'm so worried."

"What is it, Mrs. Haynes? I remember you. How is your son?"

"He's desperately ill, Mr. Cayce, in Murray Hill Hospital here in New York. He was operated on for ruptured appendix on Tuesday night, and it's turned into peritonitis. The doctors think there is only a slight chance he'll pull through!"

Cayce replied, "I'll give him a reading right away!" Then he added, "Call back in forty-five minutes!"

As she took the stairs once more to the second floor, Lila was almost smiling. At least, she felt a certain serenity she had not felt awhile ago. She thought that it would be wonderful to be able to tell Vivian that at this very moment, Mr. Cayce was preparing to give a reading for Phil. She would suggest that they pray together for the next half hour.

At the head of the stairs she met Dr. Tonner, one of Phil's attending physicians. He recognized her and stopped. "Did Dr. Dawson tell you about your son?" He added, "He's mighty bad off."

"Yes. But maybe there's hope for him yet."

Dr. Tonner looked at her sharply. Perhaps she was breaking under the strain. He would have to watch her.

"You see," Lila began, almost light-heartedly. But before she could explain, Vivian came out of Phil's room. The three of them walked to the waiting room and sat down. "Doctor," said Vivian, "please tell me what Phil was trying to say when you came in awhile ago."

Lila glanced inquiringly at the doctor. He was not as cautious as Dr. Dawson. He said, "I'll tell you, as I don't believe in holding back such things. He said that he did not want to live."

Lila gasped. "My Phil said *that?*"

"Those were his very words. He was not himself, of course. He hardly knew what he was saying."

Vivian and Lila looked at each other in disbelief. Vivian's young face was a white mask. Lila's sagged with the age she had not shown before. She thought, If he doesn't want to live, the reading will do him no good! One must *want* to live, to fight, or no treatment can help very much.

It was with all the strength she could muster that she stood up, remembering the "appointment" with Cayce and her intention to cooperate with him by keeping a time of prayer. It was this that kept her from sinking into utter despair.

"Vivian, come with me," she said. "Doctor, if we are quiet, may we sit in Phil's room for awhile?"

"Certainly. Just don't try to rouse him. He needs rest."

"We promise. We will be very quiet."

The doctor left them, and they returned to Phil's bedside. He was much as they had left him. He lay halfway between waking and sleeping, and they did nothing to disturb him.

In a low voice Lila told Vivian about her call to Cayce and of the reading he was to give this very hour. "We must keep our appointment with him, you see, in prayer." Vivian nodded and bowed her head gratefully.

At seven o'clock Lila left the room and telephoned Cayce once more. His voice was reassuring. "We can read it to you now. It was short, but very good, I think," he told her.

Now Gertrude's voice broke in and she said, "Mrs. Haynes, after the physical suggestions, Mr. Cayce said:

'We have the body here. Conditions are serious. The sepses have advanced some. The vitality is low. The resistance is low. Yet we find the *will,* the determination are strong with the inner forces of the body, and that those administrations being made are very good. We would give that, as a stimulus—through tomorrow, especially— Golden Seal or Life Everlasting, in small quantities, will aid.

"The will, the attention, the prayers of many will have the greater effect. We are through." (102-1)

As the reading was repeated, Lila wrote it down word for word; when it was ended, she thanked Gertrude with all her heart. "I'll read it to him right away, as soon as they let me," she said.

With the precious notes in her hand, she went back up the stairs to Phil's room. He was somewhat awake and saw her. He lifted his hand in greeting. Vivian stood by, saying little but imploring Lila with her eyes to bring hope to them all. Lila took his hand. Dr. Dawson had come in. "You may talk to him a little."

"Hello, Phil. I want to read something to you."

"What is it, Mother?"

"I have received a reading about you and for you from Edgar Cayce in Virginia Beach. Would you like to hear it?"

"If you think it's good, go ahead."

"All right." In her low voice she recounted the message, and it seemed to Vivian that it sounded something like a poem. When Lila was through, Phil said with a flicker of vitality, "It sounds right. It's true. I know it's all true."

"Do you want to get well, Phil?" asked Vivian.

He almost lifted his head from the pillow. "You bet I do!" His glance locked with hers. *"Now I want to live!"*

The small quantities of Golden Seal or Life Everlasting prescribed as the sole medication in the brief reading were administered that evening and through the following day. By the next day he was able to retain food, which he had not done since the operation. He had been nauseated and had vomited a good deal, but now that was over.

At the same time, Lila determined to take the entire reading to heart. She would, she told Vivian, do just what it told them. Phil's response to the reading had been so plain. The response was so real! There should be many praying for him! They should be good church men, men of faith. She went to the telephone once more and called her good friend, the Reverend deBose, who had baptized Phil into the Methodist Church when he was two. Rev. deBose quickly agreed to telephone several other ministers, including the Rev. Garrett, pastor of the First Baptist Church. They would, he said, call others and come to Phil's side as soon as possible. Among their friends, said Mr. deBose, were a priest and a rabbi.

There strode from the elevator a few hours later a lean-faced rabbi with waving dark hair who wore heavy black-rimmed glasses and a grave air about him. He was perhaps 48. He did not smile, but there was a look on his face that invited confidence.

Lila met him in the hallway, saying, "Oh, Rabbi Steiner, I'm so grateful to you." She extended her hand, and he took it warmly.

"Where is your son?"

"In here. Oh, did Dr. Dawson tell you how ill he is?"

"Yes. But he is alive. We will begin our appeal to God who is Father of us all."

"He is truly that. And you are indeed our friend. Please come into the room."

Rabbi Steiner walked into the room quietly and took a stance by the window. He watched Phil for a long moment before he closed his eyes and began to pray softly in Hebrew. Lila bowed her head, not understanding the words, but joining her own prayers with his silently.

When the prayer was over, she heard footsteps down the hall. Someone was coming—slowly, regally. It seemed to take a long time. Lila left the room to await the newcomer, thinking, "I've never called on a Catholic priest to save me or my loved ones before. Nor a rabbi."

Then Father Martinelli emerged from the depths of the hall with great dignity, and she thought of the centuries of the Catholic Church that sat upon his broad shoulders. He approached with a beautiful look of benefaction for her, taking her hand in both of his own great palms. It was, she thought, like being sheltered in the heart of a massive cathedral. He said, "Dear Mrs. Haynes, I believe?"

"Yes, Father Martinelli. Phil, my son, is in this room." She led the way and he entered slowly, taking in the sleeping form on the bed, the barren walls, the rabbi who stood contemplatively by the window.

The two men stepped toward each other with outstretched hands and greeted each other as two people intent on saving a life by appealing to a common God. Phil slept on, unaware of them, and Lila thought that all of the world lay there, in Phil, waiting for the men of faith to meet in its behalf.

Presently, Rev. deBose and Rev. Garrett entered. The first was elderly, tall, lean, with greying hair and a merry look in his eyes that spoke of many Methodist fellowship dinners. There was, too, something of the circuit rider about him, as if he had just come in from a long trek across country and was expecting to conduct a tent meeting within the hour. He grasped her hand and said, "I guess we're all here now! What a wonderful thing! Rabbi Steiner, how are you? And Father Martinelli—you beat us here!"

Young Rev. Garrett, looking ruddy-cheeked and gloriously calm, glanced often at Phil, who was about his own age. Only his eyes betrayed his inner concern. Lila's heart went out to him because of that, and because he was strong and healthy as Phil had once been. The youthful Baptist cleric was quick to sense the rapport among them and between himself and Lila. He looked into her face with earnest good will and said, "God bless you, Mrs. Haynes."

The six of them, including Vivian, now stood in a circle about the bed and bowed their heads. "Our Heavenly Father," began Reverend deBose solemnly, "we come to Thee from many paths this night, in order to ask your healing Presence here. Please be with young Phillip Haynes now as he takes on once more the will to live and to serve his fellow man. We know that he is only waiting thy loving touch and that if it is Thy will that he live, that he lives for a purpose. Be with his wife and his mother and strengthen them in this anxious time. In thy name we pray. Amen."

During this time, the prayer group led by Edgar Cayce was also praying for Phil.

From that night, Phil had progressed until at last he was able to leave the hospital. Now he was advised by later readings to recuperate at the Cayce Hospital in Virginia Beach, since his system still held the effects of the poisons from the original condition. He was admitted to the Cayce Hospital on May 29, 1930, nearly two months from the time he had been stricken. His reading that day stated that "There is a great deal of difference" in Phil's general condition from that of two months before. Although he had improved, it would be necessary to bring about proper blood coagulation and the building up of his system. He was to exercise cautiously in the open and to partake of a blood- and nerve-building diet. He was to take green vegetables in particular.

To the question, "What may be applied externally to the wound to aid healing?" Cayce replied: "We wouldn't apply anything as yet! Get the system properly adjusted and the healing will come, as has just been given, from the inside." (102-2)

Packs and antiseptics were used to heal the wound, of course. Several weeks later, Phil was well enough to ask when he could return to the work of practicing osteopathy.

"In a week or ten days. Do not attempt . . . to overtax self by too heavy work, for *osteopathy* is real work, if done properly." (102-3)

Movements involved in playing golf and tennis, which Phil asked about, would be good as long as he didn't deplete his energies. He was warned to take iodine- and calcium-containing foods and not too much potash or condiments which would put too much weight in certain places rather than in general areas. Phil, said this message, would be "a pretty good size man."

On July 17, 1930, Phil wrote to Edgar Cayce: "I am now back in my office for the first time since March and I am so happy to be here again. My health is fine—I feel quite well in all respects and hope to regain my practice in a short while.

"I simply cannot express my thanks for all the wonderful things you have done for me. My stay at the Cayce Hospital was a Godsend—I picked up so much valuable strength . . ."

Later he wrote, "I will always be interested in Cayce Hospital and if your plans change and you need me down there I hope you will call on me."

In a letter several years later, he stated that he believed that his recovery "was due to osteopathic treatment and the ministrations coming through Mr. Cayce." During his lifetime he treated many people who went to him with Cayce readings, according to Gladys Davis Turner's note in the files. He always reported favorable results, she adds.

He wrote after recovery that he was taking care of his practice and recalled that Cayce had said that osteopathy was hard work! "But the most wonderful thing that the readings did for me was to turn the tide when I lay near death in the hospital . . . That was the turning point. And I have been going upward ever since."

Medical Commentary: Peritonitis, Gangrene

by William A. McGarey, M.D.

The turning point in an illness is recognized as that timeless moment when—for one of many reasons—a sick person stops getting sicker and starts getting well. We tend to look at it as the progression of illness being stopped, when in reality it is what might best be called the re-vivification of a human being. Hope might be the instrument of change; today we depend on antibiotics more than hope. There is a restoration of balance within the body—in any event, the life force present within every one of us finds a resurgence of energy and power—and the sick person suddenly starts getting well. It is just that sudden and sometimes that simple.

No doctor who has dealt with the acutely ill has failed to see someone take a dramatic "turn" for the better, and then come rapidly alive again, gaining strength in a manner never expected. The opposite, of course, happens just as frequently, if not more so, when one who seems to be doing well suddenly changes and succumbs, leaving the physician often with the question in his mind: "What *really* happened inside that body—what *really* caused his death?" Answers to these questions are not easy to come by. We do not know, frankly, what occurs in the flow of life, the movement of all those wonderful forces within the body, that might trigger a sudden change in direction. Almost instantaneously, the dying patient suffuses with life, and his destination is obviously among those of us who are still physically present in this world rather than the other side of life—whatever that may be.

The story of this young osteopathic physician, Phil Haynes, and his peritonitis following a ruptured and apparently very septic appendicitis points out for us just this problem. That his course changed from a dismal and nearly hopeless prognosis to one of rapid recovery is the most interesting facet of this man's story. He needed care afterward, certainly, as the surgical site granulated in and closed—he was cared for in the Cayce Hospital in Virginia Beach and in time returned to his practice. These records are available and make interesting reading. The most intriguing question still remains however—what really did happen inside Phil Haynes as he passed the turning point?

Cayce was correct here, of course, in his analysis of the situation. He reassured the young man, told him he would get better, that he had the will to live, that he should take Golden Seal tea to quiet down the intestinal tract, and that he would benefit from the prayers of many. It is interesting that Cayce combined medical clairvoyance and precognition with therapeutic suggestions aimed at the mind (the suggestion that Phil wanted to live), the body (the Golden Seal tea), and the spirit (the prayers of many).

Perhaps it was the fact that Phil was given a message from an unconscious mind—something that many of us stand in awe of. He was told he had the will to live. He was already receptive, and he believed the statement, the suggestion. He *did* have the will—he *would* get well. This might have been the progression of events, and all the other factors might be of no real consequence. Suggestion is a powerful tool, and it would certainly work better coming from one like Cayce than from his own mother or wife. With the history of hypnosis to draw from, one cannot exclude this as a possibility, as the sole cause of recovery.

We must also look at the possibility that Phil in reality did have the will to live, even before Cayce pointed it out to him in the reading. Perhaps the reading came at a time when the change was starting anyway. Perhaps he would have gotten well without the reading. We cannot say otherwise, even though the prognosis was dark and the patient was not doing well. And the stomach might have quieted down without the tea. All these possibilities should be looked at and considered. To go back forty years and reconstruct a condition of illness is difficult at best.

In all fairness, however, one must also explore the obvious sequence of events, evaluating their individual influences on the total picture of the story Mrs. Carter has given us.

Let us suppose that Cayce clairvoyantly "saw"—as he stated—that Phil Haynes had a strong determination, a strong will to live. He also pointed out that the administrations being made by the doctors were very good. He did not seem to be making a point of suggesting anything to the patient except that this was the state of affairs, and that he was in actuality going to get better. This stimulus may have been all Phil needed to recognize within himself that he really *did* want to live, and thus activate the tremendous power of will that is within each of us. In other readings Cayce has much to say about will—its strength in the lives of people and how nothing in one's experience is stronger than his will. It seems to unlock spiritual strength which can bring one back from almost certain death. It can generate unbelievable changes in one's life, as it acts to supersede the laws of the physical

87

body and its environment. The will, of course, is closely associated with the mind. In reading 416-2, Cayce said:

Let the entity understand and know—there is no urge or influence that exceeds the will. . . . For, the WILL is that factor which is the birthright of each soul, each entity, through which choice is made, and by which the entity exercises that prerogative of showing itself to be a child of God with the abilities to apply spiritual influences rather than merely the exercising of natural or nature's laws in its relationships to Creative Forces.

Cayce's next suggestion was the only one having to do with the body. He suggested that Phil be given Golden Seal tea in small quantities as a stimulant, as an aid to the body. As he took the tea the vomiting and nausea ceased—certainly, in the early thirties, a necessary step in the recuperative process, even as it is today. Modern therapy, with antibiotics, drugs, and intravenous injections, would seldom leave a patient in as much distress as Phil found himself. These things, however, were not available.

Golden Seal is an herb, the root of the plant *Hydrastis canadensis*. It is known by a wide variety of other names, such as yellow paint root, orange root, Indian paint, yellow eye, and jaundice root. It is held in highest esteem by those who are knowledgeable about herbs. It has been used over the ages externally as a relief for skin problems and internally for a multitude of things, particularly for inflamed conditions of the stomach and small intestine. The root itself is classified medically as a hemostatic and astringent, but it is rarely employed as such. The alkaloids having similar hemostatic and astringent qualities, hydrastine, berberine, and canadine, are extracted from the *Hydrastis*.

The patient was given an ancient therapy and his intestinal tract responded, his nausea ceased, and he then was able once again to take nourishment so important to the recovery process.

We are told that prayer interceded for Phil. The mother in the case was not a hesitant woman. She covered the field—Baptist, Methodist, Catholic, Jew. Ministers, priest, and rabbi stood together with Phil's wife and mother, following the heritage of the Judeo-Christian faith of the ages, asking God for a physical healing. Is such a healing possible? Members of the medical profession have attested to sudden, miraculous healings that have occurred at Lourdes, France, for most of the decades of this century. So many documented recoveries have been recorded all over the world that it no longer is reasonable to comment until one has at least become familiar with the field. Kathryn Kuhlman has been an outstanding figure in this field since the middle 1940's. The relationship of prayer to healing of the physical body is a fact. We need to find out what happens.

In the case of Phil Haynes, the members of the clergy—and others—participated in what Cayce gave as the summation of his reading: "The will, the attention, the prayers of many will have the greater effect."

So what was it that actually brought about the turn of events which saw Phil move from illness toward recovery? As Cayce saw it, there are many channels through which healing might come. He saw all life as a oneness. No matter how an individual is able to bring to the awareness of the cells within his body that they *are* one with Creative Energy which we call God, healing comes when that awareness is accomplished. Thus, healing could come through the mind, the body, the spirit of man, since they are one. The prayers, the awakening of the will, the administrations by the doctors—all might bring healing. Healing, Cayce said, is all of the same source, whether it be the laying on of hands, the use of medicine, herbs, surgery, or prayer—all healing comes from God.

A great many of us are skeptical. We need reasons and explanations. Cayce apparently had this in mind when he gave the following reading:

Let's analyze healing for a moment, for the benefit of those who, like this body, must consciously see and reason—see a material demonstration, occasionally, at least!

Each atomic force of a physical body is made up of its units of positive and negative forces, which bring it into a material plane. These are of the ether, or atomic forces, which are electrical in nature when they enter into materiality or become matter, with its ability to take on or throw off.

A group may thus raise those atomic vibrations which make for *positive* forces, which bring divine force into action in a material plane—*destructive* forces are broken down by the raising of that vibration! That's a "material explanation," see? And this is accomplished through Creative Forces, which are God in manifestation! (281-3)

Keeping things in context, then, Cayce was internally consistent in his readings as he unconsciously surveyed the situation, saw that only a few things were really needed. He suggested that these be done; and the sick man changed, turned the corner, and began to find health again.

Grandmother Takes A Hand

by Mary Ellen Carter

Tears welled in the eyes of 13-month-old Jane Marsh. She rubbed her ears fretfully, for the cold she had been having during the past week had settled in them.

Alicia, her mother, decided to take her to the family physician. Upon examining Jane, he thought it best to puncture both her ears in an attempt to cure the infection that had developed. But Jane grew worse, and he prescribed a new medicine.

It was the Sunday before Christmas, 1932, when Betty, her grandmother, took a hand in helping to care for her. In a letter to Edgar Cayce afterward, Betty wrote: "When I started to give her the second dose [of the prescribed medicine] she cried so hard that I only gave her half of it. I took the balance, myself, as a test. I found it contained something which burned terribly.

"In less than two hours from that time she began to break out in splotches on the lower limbs, and the bottoms of her feet had dark spots on them."

91

When Jane was touched on her legs, she cried. At midnight, when the doctor was again called in, he said that this was "a form of hives." When he learned that the medicine burned so severely, he ordered it discontinued.

"If that baby is living tomorrow morning," Betty told her husband that night, "I'm going to get Mr. Cayce to give a reading for her if possible." She added, "In all my years of child raising, I've never seen anything like those symptoms."

Jane now had dark circles around her ankles; her ears were black except for the lobes. Even the soles of her feet were black.

The next morning, they called in a specialist. He found her gums looked "mortified," to use the report in the readings from Betty's account.

The reading, 324-1, given immediately at Betty's request, was telephoned to her by Miss Gladys Davis, a personal friend of the Cayce family. Betty said nothing of the reading to the specialist, for it indicated, she said, that the treatments outlined wouldn't interfere with anything already being done.

With her daughter's grateful cooperation, Betty followed both the specialist's treatment and the reading. "The specialist prescribed only something to make a lining in her stomach where the medicine had destroyed the tissue to a certain extent; a sedative for making her sleep; and a mouth wash. The child's temperature registered 104½ degrees, yet these were all the specialist ordered," according to Betty.

"As we find," began Jane's first reading, "there are the effects of cold and congestion, especially to the membranes of the throat and head; that is, the effect that produces such an amount of temperature.

"That to be prevented most is this causing too great a strain on the soft tissue, as to produce antrum or the ear trouble, or descending into the bronchi and lungs and making for the inflammation of the pleural cavity.

"While the temperature is high, as we find, some little

92

changes in the ministrations would make for better conditions for the body."

The reading recommended the following treatment:

"First, we would massage as much camphorated oil in the spine, chest, and throat as the body will take up.

"We would massage the soles of the feet with mutton tallow, camphor, and turpentine. Keep these very warm. These would be mixed in proportions as about equal parts of each, see? Necessary, then, of course, to dissolve the mutton tallow. Two or three drops of the spirits of camphor and spirits of turpentine to about twice the amount of the mutton tallow dissolved. Of course, do not have this so hot as to burn, but have warm when applied and keep wrapped in hot flannels.

"We would take the syrup of squill, five to eight drops every three to four hours.

"Dissolve five grains of calcidin in ten ounces of water. Keep warm, and every few minutes when there is the choking or the irritating of the body give a few sips of this, see?

"These may be given without fear of hindering or being effective with any other applications.

"Do that.

"The oil and the squill, especially, will reduce the temperature.

"Be mindful of this, especially through the coming night and morning."

When the question about nourishment was asked, the answer came that nourishment was to be kept, but that they should not permit cold or congestion to settle in the lungs or upon the intestinal system as to cause colitis or any of the disorders from same. Hence, pre-digested foods would be better and natural fruit juices, with no sugar.

"Should all other treatments now being applied be kept up?"

"Only when necessary, for if these are applied properly,

we will see—in four to six hours—a great deal of change for the better."

Later that day, a neighbor came over to see Jane. She looked at the tiny form in the crib and shook her head. "I've only seen two people in that condition," she said sadly.

"Did they get over it?" Betty asked, a bit shaken.

The mournful visitor hesitated uncomfortably. "No, they didn't."

Betty refused to be dismayed. "Here's one that is going to get well!" she smiled.

She followed the treatments scrupulously, massaging the little chest and spine and throat with the strong-smelling oil; rubbing the small feet with warm mutton tallow, camphor, turpentine; and following all the rest of the instructions. Just as the reading had promised, Jane's temperature began to drop at about 7 o'clock that evening! Betty and Alicia were overjoyed. Sharing their joy was Miss Davis, who had arrived for a visit to the little patient.

When the specialist came the next morning, Betty showed him the chart she had kept of Jane's temperature drop. He was amazed. "Well," he said, "I expected to find her *some* better . . ."

"As I never told him about the reading," Betty relates, "he never knew what brought it all about."

The sign of the "hives" had for the most part disappeared, and, with the temperature dropping, the outlook was much better. Grandmother Betty, in her exhilaration over the improvement of her grandchild, became a little lax in her applications of the treatments Cayce had suggested. The result? The minute she relaxed the treatments, Jane's temperature would begin to rise! When she resumed them, it fell.

The specialist could not understand the fluctuation. A blood test which he took proved negative, so he called in another specialist who took a Malta fever test. This, too, was negative.

Within a week, Jane was out of danger. She recovered

completely except for the right ear, which would start to discharge again whenever she got the least bit of a cold. This continued for the next three or four months. Her grandmother requested a second reading, given April 28, 1933, which answered questions about the infectious forces still present, especially in her right ear. For this, Cayce prescribed one drop of a mixture of St. Jacob's oil diluted with sweet oil, warmed, just before bedtime. The ear should be cleansed in the morning with an antiseptic solution, he added. Jane's system should be cleansed at this time with Fletcher's Castoria "with added senna." Her feet should be given daily massage with small quantities of olive oil and tincture of myrrh for an infection located on her foot.

The following September, Betty reported that Jane became completely well in response to the treatment faithfully carried out.

Medical Commentary: Ear Infection

by William A. McGarey, M.D.

This is a rather simple story, but it does have certain implications and ramifications which should be explored. The response of the modern physician would most likely be that a simple antihistamine preparation and an antibiotic would have prevented the complications and rendered this a very mild infection, perhaps not *even* necessitating the surgical care to the eardrums. And certainly the recurring ear infection would not likely have come about. In 1943, however, antihistamines and antibiotics were a thing of the future, and the problem facing these people was a matter of life and death. A severe urticaria involving the entire body can be a frightful thing, and the problem facing the doctor at that point with the armamentarium at his command was a difficult one.

In his reading given for this child, Cayce saw the possibility of Jane's sickness being complicated by mastoid trouble, bronchitis, pneumonia, and possibly colitis, if the infection were not controlled. This is, in the medical mind, a reasonable—though psychic—insight on the part of Mr. Cayce.

The story of this very ill little infant highlights, in my mind, the question of the proper doctor-patient relationship. Why did the mother and the grandmother not tell the doctors about having a psychic reading done for the child's benefit? Were they afraid of being rebuffed and ridiculed because they asked the advice of someone with only Cayce's credentials? It seems reasonable to me that any physician worthy of the name should be willing to learn more about the nature of the body—knowing as we do so little about it. Should they have been hesitant?

A partial answer to these questions might be found in the life story of Edgar Cayce. Time and again he was scoffed at by the medical profession. This is unfortunate, but true. When Wesley Ketchum, M.D., for instance, actually worked with difficult patients who were given readings by Cayce and saw them improve and recover, he reported this to his fellow physicians. He, in turn, was laughed at, ridiculed, and finally threatened with expulsion from his medical society. Incidents such as this may have been influential here in the hesitancy shown in confiding the facts to the doctors.

Apparently Betty—the grandmother—did not really trust herself to tell them that she was doing other things than just what they ordered. She went ahead and did what Cayce instructed her to do, keeping this information from the family doctor and the pediatrician. Not the best relationship, this.

Perhaps this story is also an interesting little incident—vitally important to those involved in it, of course—to demonstrate that the healing of the body is not only the concern of the physician. It points up the fact that anyone who wants to be of assistance can be involved in the healing process; and that healing, which really comes from God, is not limited to the professional in the field.

This is not a new idea, of course. It is utilized every time a mother kisses the hurt on her child's knee or rubs away the pain when he bumps his elbow. It is the thought behind one person praying for another, and it underlies the love that motivates literally thousands of volunteers who help out in hospitals and clinics around the world.

Every time Cayce gave a reading, he demonstrated that one person's unconscious mind could reach out and contact the point of awareness in another person's body which knew what was wrong with that body. That was the nature of the physical readings as Cayce described them himself, repeated over and over again more than 9,000 times.

This repetitive and demonstrably accurate procedure provides us with the fascinating information that each of us—at some level of our unconscious mind—knows what is wrong with our own physical body when we are ill. This expands the realm of healing as we presently know it, for it indicates to us that perhaps there are no illnesses which cannot be diagnosed with an amazing accuracy. And it implies that were we to utilize this knowledge which is inherent within us, we might also come to know what needs to be done then to restore the body to health. Cayce apparently used the same capabilities in different ways to diagnose the problem and to prescribe for the illness. In some manner his mind reached out and contacted a source of knowledge which provided him with means to change the physiological functioning of the body more toward normal. This involves all of us in the healing act. Betty was not really astray, since she wanted to help her little granddaughter.

But what about the therapy which Cayce suggested— the treatments which apparently were instrumental in preventing complications of the infection and restoring the little girl back to a state of good health? Let's investigate these a bit more thoroughly. He suggested:

1. Massage the chest, throat, and spine with as much camphorated oil as the body will absorb. (I would imagine this was done two or three times a day.)

2. Massage the soles of the feet with equal parts of a warm mixture of mutton tallow, spirits of turpentine, and spirits of camphor, and keep the feet wrapped in hot flannel cloth. (Elsewhere in the readings, he stated that these substances should be made up beginning with heated mutton tallow, with the spirits of turpentine and camphor added in that order.)
3. Dietary advice: Eat only unsweetened, natural fruit juices and predigested foods.
4. Take syrup of squill, five to eight drops every three or four hours.
5. Take a few sips every few minutes of a mixture of five grains of calcidine in ten ounces of water as needed to relieve cough.

These procedures were obviously directed toward certain therapeutic objectives. Cayce wanted to protect the body from developing colitis while this infectious-allergic process was being dissipated. That was one of the functions of the diet prescribed. From my knowledge of these readings, I would understand the diet to be intended also to alkalinize the blood stream in the process, for natural fruit juice has that property—fruit and vegetables being the prime food substances providing an alkaline ash on analysis. Along with a number of other sources, Cayce laid great stress on an alkaline-reacting diet in infectious conditions of the body. He once stated that the body which is kept slightly alkaline in its reaction (primarily, he implied, through the diet) would not likely catch a cold. There are extremes in both acid and alkaline states of the human body, however, that are seriously detrimental.

Camphorated oil rubbed on the spine, chest and throat? This is a treatment used for years and years—not really anything new, of course. But Cayce said that this, plus the syrup of squill, would reduce the temperature. It—or something—did reduce the temperature, and in the time suggested. Why? Squill is described in the medical references as an expectorant and a diuretic and is prepared from the inner scales of the bulb of the white variety of *Urginea maritima,* a lilaceous plant. Does it have antipyretic qualities in addition?

What about the camphorated oil? It is a 20% weight solidus volume mixture of camphor oil in cottonseed oil, described as a counterirritant embrocation. This means that when it is applied to the body by rubbing, it tends to produce an inflammation of the skin for the relief of a more deep-seated irritation. We are not told *how* such a substance rubbed on the outside of the body affects irritation inside the body, but by its use over the ages, such a result has consistently come about. Thus its definition has developed while its methodology has remained unknown.

Thus, the combination of these two substances, one producing a carrying away of irritation deep in the tissues of the chest, throat, and spine, and the other acting as a diuretic—increasing certainly the elimination of substances from the body—brought about a relief of the high fever and apparently contributed to the resolution of the infection and the allergic condition which was present.

Calcidine is rarely used by the physician today. Calcidrine, as a cough preparation, is still available. The former, however, is a tablet which, when dissolved in water (adult dosage being 2½ grains in four ounces of water taken every hour during the day for four to five days if needed), was indicated for dry cough and scant secretions. It is a compound containing 15% available iodine in combination with lime and starch. It is interesting that Cayce suggested that five grains be dissolved in ten ounces of water and the mixture be given in sips as needed. This manner of administration would pass muster with the best pediatric pharmacology standards of that day.

The remaining therapeutic measure Cayce suggested to bring some degree of balance to this little child was the mutton tallow spirits of turpentine and spirits of camphor mixture. This combination was suggested in

100

literally dozens of readings given for respiratory conditions of the body. Consistently, advice was given to rub this either on the chest and throat or into the soles of the feet—sometimes after a hot foot bath and sometimes after a hot tub bath. One individual (585) was told to bring his fever down by bathing his feet in hot water every four hours and, following this, to take a rubdown from the hips to the feet. He was also told to massage the feet with the combination of mutton tallow, spirits of turpentine, and spirits of camphor.

In his reading given for the common cold (902-1) Cayce stated that the first remedy which should be applied in this condition is rest. Then treatment should be directed where the weakness lies. In most instances lack of eliminations is a major factor, and in many individuals the process of assimilation needs correction. Plenty of water is needed and, in most people, an alkalizer of the system would be in order. Something to stimulate eliminations seems to be almost a constant factor in Cayce's prescriptions

While Jane's condition was not a cold, the respiratory system was highly affected, so Cayce's generalities in reference to colds probably were at least partially brought to bear on this problem. It may be that the unusual mixture was intended just to help bring down the fever, but its use so generally in respiratory conditions of the body in the Cayce readings would rather imply that there was something of a healing influence also brought to bear within the physiological processes of the body by the administration of this strange combination of substances.

Thus, the therapy which an alert grandmother was able to administer brought about a relief of the cough, an increase in the eliminations of the body, a resolution of irritations deep within the body, an antipyretic effect, an aid (or a "booster") to assimilation, an alkalinization of the body, and a probable healing effect of unknown quality and quantity. Quite a bit of change brought to the body, if indeed all these things are operative.

This child's experience provides a good example of the manner in which the Cayce readings directed healing to come about. Not by a medication designed to eliminate an illness, but rather a group of therapies aimed at restoring the equilibrium, the balance, and coordination of the forces within the body which, when full and normal, spell health for the body.

Tell Them The Lame Walk

by Mary Ellen Carter

Mid-July of 1929 found Virginia Beach a haven for vacationers and visitors from out-of-town. It was a wonderful time and place to be young. At 19, Ginny Meades should have been at the beach with her husband Bart and their friends, as they had once been free to do. But for six months now, Ginny had been crippled and helpless from what doctors had told her was acute rheumatism. For her, especially, the joys of swimming in the surf and running on the beach were over.

Dr. Frank Johnson straightened up after examining Ginny and shook his head. She lay on the sofa, her once lovely body twisted beneath her cotton dress, her legs turned almost backward, her spine grotesquely bent. In her eyes was a mute plea for help.

He was shocked by what he had found. Her right leg had become at least ten inches shorter than the left! Her poor right knee had become so turned that the back almost faced forward.

"I'm afraid," he told Ginny's mother, who stood anxiously nearby, "that Ginny's spine is too twisted as a result of rheumatism for any hope it will ever be straight again."

At that moment Bart came in. Ginny knew from his expression that he had bad news. "Hello, Bart," she said, trying to hide the fear and anguish of that moment. When Dr. Johnson had left, she didn't at once tell him her own devastating news. Instead, she said, "You . . . didn't get the job?"

"No! But I'll try again tomorrow." He looked closely at Ginny. "What did the doctor tell you?"

When she had finished repeating Dr. Johnson's sad prediction, her lips trembled and she hid her face in the pillow. Bart put an arm around her and tried to comfort her. But the disappointment of his day had been topped by this; he could only offer an awkward kiss on her forehead. "Please don't cry," he said. But she did.

She had cried when the dull pain began in her legs last winter. The bitter damp winds that blew in from the Atlantic chilled the bones and sent one scurrying indoors. Grey clouds hovered overhead on that February day. As Ginny struggled to gather the wash from the line in her tiny backyard, she felt a pain in her legs she had never felt before. That night it became so severe that Bart called Dr. Radford, who agreed to examine Ginny in the morning. Following the examination, Dr. Radford advised that Ginny go to a hospital for treatment of acute rheumatism.

She exchanged glances with Bart. "Where will we get the money?" she asked. There seemed no answer.

Ginny suffered for a month at home before, with the help of friends and Dr. Radford, she was admitted to a Norfolk hospital. During the following weeks, she received all possible care. Three doctors attended her in addition to Dr. Radford. Her condition, however, gradually worsened. By May, her legs were beginning to swell, her spine was twisting, her right leg had grown five inches shorter than her left, she had lost her appetite.

Ginny was pronounced incurable. "I'm afraid there is nothing more we can do for you here, Ginny," Dr. Radford told her. "You may go home."

At home, Ginny's mother and two sisters nursed her, feeling certain that she would never recover. Ginny was by now so helpless that she couldn't feed herself; her appetite, however, returned as the rheumatism medicine was discontinued.

One day, Dr. Johnson came to the house to see one of Ginny's sisters. "Doctor, while you're here, would you look at our Ginny?" her mother requested. It was this visit that had led to the doctor's corroboration of the first doctor's prediction: Ginny would never walk again.

One evening shortly thereafter, Ginny and Bart discussed her plight. "Surely," said Ginny quietly, "there is somebody in this world who knows more about my problem and could tell me something to make me well again!"

As if in answer to her expression of faith, something happened soon that brought her hope. Her mother hired a painter to redecorate the house. As it was summertime, Ginny could be moved out of the house into the shade. Bill Langhorn stopped his work to ask her, "What are they doin' for you, if you don't mind my askin'?"

"Why, we don't know what to do. The doctors have given me up."

Bill's blue eyes lit up as he said slowly, "Well, ma'am, maybe there's a doctor here in town can help you."

"What do you mean?"

"A guy here claims he can help folks like you. I been doin' some work for him this past spring. He's a mighty fine man."

The day seemed to stand still. The birds had hushed, and in the distance there were the cries of children playing. "Tell me about him."

When Ginny's mother heard the story, she said, "There

are many strange things in this world. And I'm going to find out about this one!"

That afternoon she made her way to the two-story house at 115 West 35th Street where she introduced herself and told Edgar Cayce her problem. The next day, Edgar came to see Ginny, accompanied by Dr. Thomas B. House, head of the Cayce Hospital. Dr. House examined her and said, "I can see why you were given up."

Ginny thought that she had never met two more kindly men. When they left, she had their assurance that Edgar would give her a reading. "But I don't know if I can help or not. I will try," Edgar cautioned.

Ginny's first reading was given the day following, July 19, at 3:30 in the afternoon. It was to be one of 45 physical readings she would receive over the next ten years. It referred to conditions stemming from two causes: one "of long standing" which brought to mind, Ginny later recalled, a fall four years before; and "disturbances in the structural portion of the system."

Trouble in her white blood leukocytes had "allowed the bone structure about the clavicle and fibre to form that of a seepage that has brought about enlarging of the bone, itself." (This was later called by other doctors "Osteochondritis or Perthe's disease," according to a notation by Gladys Davis Turner.) The condition was indicated by "the character of the plasm in the red blood cell," as well. It could be corrected, Cayce advised, by doses of carbon ash in distilled water; then ultra-violet ray on her body twice a week.

"First, we must stop the inroads of these conditions produced by this seepage. Then, we must create in the system, in the blood supply, that building force that will so build about it such cartilaginous forces as to aid the body in having sufficient strength" for the use of her shortened and twisted right leg. He promised that she would be able to walk, eventually, without the aid of crutches, depending on how her body responded to the treatment. (409-1)

Ginny was admitted to the Cayce Hospital on July 31 by Dr. Grace C. Berger, D.O., to be treated for a dislocated hip. On August 15, a check reading suggested that as the swelling and seepage from the bone joint were allayed, and the soreness had left, she should now begin to force the use of her limbs as fast as possible. The treatments should be continued and osteopathic treatment should be given gently after the soreness was gone. (409-2) By September 23, she was to have, not merely gentle massage, but deep manipulations, especially in the lumbar and sacral region and in the lower dorsal to relieve pressure on her kidneys. "We would begin also with the gradual pushing down of the bone in the hip, so that the *muscular* forces—as they are relaxed through the sacral and lumbar—may be brought into play, near their normal or correct position." (409-3) She should continue the ultra-violet ray. It would relieve the tendency of inflammation from the manipulations. By October, she was to use a crutch and cane.

This was a great advancement from the pitiful condition she had presented upon her arrival five months before! Her first steps were hailed by the staff with joy. To her, it seemed a miracle.

Care had to be taken, she was warned in a reading, that there be little strain on her side muscles because these were directly connected with the errant bone. The lengthening of her leg, to be aided by exercise and manipulation, would be disconcerting at first.

Adjustments were now given involving weights on her right leg. In November, she was told that she should have oil and myrrh rubs. The bone was gradually taking its correct position and it would remain that way.

Before leaving for a few days' visit home, she hobbled about the hospital to practice walking with her cane. When she arrived at home, Bart and her mother watched anxiously. She laughed. "I can walk," she told them.

Ginny was, in fact, the hospital's "star patient." Edgar took a special interest in her, giving her moral support during the long months, having encouraging talks with Bart. Of course, they had at times been very depressed, with Ginny feeling that Bart was neglecting her if he didn't come to visit as often as she thought he should. Now, all that seemed to be passed. On November 29, Edgar wrote a friend: "It was very nice to see Mrs. Meades coming in from a visit home this a.m., walking into the hospital (with her crutch, of course) when we remember how it was when she was brought in first."

Like all hospitals, the Cayce Hospital depended upon the fees it charged its patients as well as upon donations. But Ginny had no money at all, so she was taken in as a charity patient. All she could give was her willingness to cooperate with the treatments. As her case is a triumphant one in the Cayce files, this proved to be a valuable contribution. Without her own valiant efforts, she would have remained a cripple.

She continued to heal. Her foot, she wrote later, "stretched a little each day until I was able to touch the floor."

After returning to the hospital, she was encouraged now in a reading to add the "deeper rays, or infra-red rays" to her system. She should precede this with hot packs or wet packs for five to ten minutes before the treatments of manipulation and rays. The packs would relax her body. She was warned that stiffness in her back and soreness in ankle and foot might result unless this was done properly. Oil rubs were to be given "more systematically and thoroughly, especially in the ends of sinews, or in the joints of the foot, ankle, knee, and hip." She was to persist in stretching her foot. She should take her exercises on the porch to benefit from the sparkling air and sunlight. At this point she began using two canes instead of a crutch and a cane. By early spring, 1930, she walked with only one cane.

By May, she was certain she could walk alone. Finally, the day came when the doctors told her that she might walk without help. She had been tapping gamely about the premises, in her head bright pictures of Bart and herself running on the beach again like children, swimming and dancing. When the hour arrived for her to leave, the hospital staff and the ambulatory patients crowded around to see her off. With a smile she stood on the porch and handed her cane to Dr. Berger. A cheer went up from everyone! It was a time to remember, one which Edgar smilingly watched, no doubt seeing about Ginny just then an aura of gold.

Check readings every month thereafter until 1932 led her safely back to complete normalcy and freedom from pain. However, she had become overactive after leaving the hospital and was advised in a reading to go to Richmond for a surgical operation. She was there for three months, in a cast for eight weeks. At home, she resumed treatments suggested in the readings and attained full recovery by January, 1932, when she wrote: "I feel that I owe my life to the work of Mr. Edgar Cayce and all that I can ever say will express only in a small measure my deep appreciation and thankfulness that I was privileged to contact him in this time of dire need; for he showed me the way when all human agencies had apparently failed. I feel that this is a God-given gift worthy of consideration, and those who will follow his suggestions as I have followed them will reap the same wonderful results.

"I shall be glad to answer any questions about my case."

Ginny not only was cured of crippling rheumatism, she had gained new spiritual insight and knowledge of God's mercy. She wrote in January, 1932: "My last check reading informed me that I would be proud of myself in time, which I certainly am!"

In subsequent years, her devotion to the work was expressed by her influencing others among her family and friends to go to Edgar Cayce in times of stress. At least seven of these are on record. One day, she was at the hospital when a patient was waiting for his reading. "Be sure and follow it faithfully," she told him.

Ginny Meades died at the age of 30 of acute dropsy which apparently developed following pneumonia, according to her medical record. But for ten years, thanks to Edgar Cayce, she walked.

Medical Commentary: Perthe's Disease

by William A. McGarey, M.D.

In twenty-five years of practicing medicine, I have never seen a case of Legg-Calvé-Perthes disease of this severity. The right leg was out of joint at the hip, foreshortened by a full ten inches and rotated so that the knee cap and toes pointed more backward than forward. There was apparently drainage from a chronic suppurative osteochondritis, and the patient had a scoliosis that rendered her— with the other deformities—completely unable to care for herself.

Today, in most instances, treatment of a surgical nature would intervene with this kind of a problem and bring about at least a partial resolution. Things do not often go as far as this case. *Osteochondritis deformans* still has a frustrating and disappointing outlook for the victim and the immediate family, however, since even reconstructive surgery has its limits on the one hand and its failures on the other.

This particular case is an excellent example of what

medical care plus osteopathy plus physical therapy can do. Perhaps the most fascinating aspect of this whole series of readings is this simple illustration that more can be done with the physical body in the way of total rehabilitation than most of us really accept at the present time as being possible. Perhaps this is an ideal example of what happens when therapy is aimed at restoring, regenerating, and rebuilding the various functions of the body while maintaining a balance that we have come to know as homeostasis.

Homeostasis in the human body is that balance of energies, functions, and structures that allows the continuity of the life process. It fits into the Cayce concept of things in that homeostasis is the balance that the life force within the body creates so that the spiritual being that we call man might live in this three-dimensional sphere and fulfill the purpose for which he came into being.

Ginny—in this story—was a constant problem, however, in that she apparently had a major degree of difficulty in assisting the healing process from the standpoint of emotions and mental attitudes. The effect of emotional turmoil and negative attitudes was commented on again and again in the readings given for this young lady, since the balance of life forces was often difficult indeed to achieve within her body. She must have had a tumultuous unconscious mind with emotional patterns that would come unhinged at the slightest urging.

But the healing progressed, sometimes in spite of the emotions, and the patterns of therapy suggested through this unconscious source of information are like the weaving of a tapestry. A certain effect is achieved only after a period of time and effort. Ginny spent many months in the Cayce Hospital, received an inordinate amount of care it seems, but achieved a truly remarkable result.

It is not really an unheard of thing to see the regeneration of the bone and cartilege of the hip joint. Medical

112

literature[1] records the case of a woman who underwent the almost complete regeneration of her hip joint over a four-year period when she had the sympathetic nerves to her hip joint and leg area sectioned. X-rays before and after revealed the results of the regenerative effort the body accomplished.

But to work with the adrenal-sympathetic complex still intact, with the femur out of joint at the hip—this is even more remarkable. It would have been most interesting to have seen x-ray progression of this series of events over the time period which elapsed between Cayce's visit to Ginny's home and Ginny's walk out of the hospital under her own steam, with the head of the femur back in its proper place.

The cause of Perthes' disease is not clear in the reference books of medical science. Neither did Cayce render the question crystal clear in his comments. He did give us a few ideas, however, which might be worth considering.

It seems that Ginny's white blood cells were inadequate in numbers—she had a leukopenia. There was also present what Cayce called an abnormal character of the red cell plasm. Perhaps this means that the red blood cells were not exactly healthy in their nature. At one point, there apparently was an injury, and the bone underwent injury which might be called an infraction, or perhaps incomplete fracture. And, in the process of repair, the body was unable, because of the cellular components of the blood and their inadequacies, to bring about a full callus formation.

Where the bone had failed to heal properly, there occurred a seepage or drainage; and this, in turn, caused the structural portion of the body to suffer:

"This instability about the blood supply has allowed the

[1] W. H. Cammerer, and T. I. Hoen, "Unexpected Radiographic Changes of the Hip Joint Following Lumbar Sympathectomy for Arthritis," *Arthritis & Rheumatism*, Vol. 10, No. 3, p. 288, June 1967.

bone structure . . . and fibre to form that of a seepage that has brought about enlarging of the bone itself. This, then, is that as produces distress and creating in the system those conditions as bring abnormalities for the body." (53-1)

This "seepage," as Cayce called it, was a constant drain on the body energies and posed an ever-present problem in the therapeutic program. Ginny needed to stem this energy drain in order to bring about gradual repair.

The etiology, then, seemed to be an injury superimposed on an inadequate body repair system—the failure of union within the bone bringing about the toxic effect to the entire body that caused the progression of events that led to the young lady's terrible plight at the time of her first reading.

In analyzing the measures suggested to bring about a restorative process within this girl's body, one is faced with the obvious fact that he must deal with general objectives rather than specifics and with the constant need to maintain a balance that will support a regenerative effort. This suits the objectives of a physical therapy department much more aptly than the desires of an internist —broad objectives rather than specific therapeutic results.

As I see it, there were five basic goals in Cayce's therapeutic program:

1. To stop the seepage from the injured bone
2. To build up the body generally, especially the formed elements of the blood stream, e.g., the white and red blood cells
3. To keep the balance of the body intact as much as possible as changes came about
4. To create in the system a "building force" that would in turn bring about the regeneration of the bone and cartilage of the joint and the strength for using the limb thus resuscitated
5. To use a variety of physical therapy modalities to bring about the gradual stretching of the tendons,

the relocation of the femur in its hip socket, and the strengthening of the muscles and ligaments and tendons that are involved in the diseased area

Cayce's language is sometimes poetic in its expression but at other times a complete enigma—or so it seems. He states the therapeutic direction in a way, however, that bears repeating, since it relates the objectives sought for in a manner that gives them coherence and perhaps gives us a better understanding.

First we must stop the *inroads* of those conditions produced by this seepage. Then we must create in the system, in the blood supply, that building force that will so build about it such cartilaginous forces as to aid the body in having sufficient strength for the use of same through that limb, see? (409-1)

Cayce further stated that Ginny's condition might be materially aided if applications are made

... for the correction of those conditions that will so build in the general physical forces those properties as will meet the needs of the condition and hinder or ward off, or encase, those conditions where seepage has occurred from this fracture as has existed, to such an extent as to allow the usage [of the limb]; as well as preventing the inroads and the creating of that condition in the structural portion itself as to create that as will build within itself the deficiencies for the normal action of the body (409-1)

How did the actual therapy progress in the hospital, once started? The ultra-violet ray was used regularly for months. Later on, the infra-red lamp was used. She was taken out on the beach near the hospital where she absorbed the sunlight and received the benefit of the sands.

Massage was a constant therapy—designed gently at first to stretch the tendons and ease spasms, to bring about a better lymph flow and stimulate the healing process.

115

Later on, the massage was deeper and stronger and osteopathic manipulation was added to the regimen. Traction was used in various forms to stretch the muscles and gradually make possible the replacing of the femur head into its socket.

Care was taken to prevent infections, such as respiratory problems, as these would hinder the progress of general repair. Diet was always a part of the treatment for those who were patients in the Cayce Hospital. The patient was given an alkaline-reacting diet, was kept from rich foods and was given those foods high in vitamins and similar food values.

Carbon ash was given through the mouth to this girl over a long period of time. This was the ash deposited on the globe of a carbon arc lamp burned in a partial vacuum. Cayce attributed to this fine dust or ash a value which he described as a power of oxygenation of the blood stream and tissues of the body, especially if given just before the use of the ultra-violet lamp. He said the use of the ash would tend to stop the seepage.

The program certainly was not one of bizarre therapies or unusual procedures. Aside from the ash, the treatments could have been given by any physician trained in his art. But it encompassed time and patience and demanded consistency and persistence. These qualities are hard to come by in one person, or, for that matter, in a group of persons. Ginny was making progress but felt after five months of continuous treatments that the hip should be getting back to normal soon. So she asked the question in her sixth reading given in November, still in the hospital:

Q. How long before it [the hip] will be normal?
A. Dependent upon the applications and how the body applied itself, and what accidents would or may happen to the body, and how the care is taken of the whole system. That's the same as to say when will a fly be swatted or when will it miss being hit!

116

Patience was apparently not one of her strong points. We are not given a clear picture of just how the mental-emotional pattern present here actually interfered with the therapy, or just what Ginny's emotional hang-up was. Apparently, however, there was such a hang-up. One night Cayce himself had to quiet down the sick girl from a crying and weeping episode when her husband had not come in to visit her for a time.

As her stay in the hospital wore on, the treatments continued under Cayce's unconscious guidance, but a warning crept into the very short reading given in April —after eight months of hospitalization. Ginny was told that the time had come when she could exercise more if she were to take proper precautions.

. . . but will the body be indiscreet in its actions, in its diet, in its moral and physical life, it may expect the latter condition worse than the first. Now choose! We are through. (409-11)

In all the philosophy of health, illness, and healing that came through this very unusual source, there was always the bare fact that emotions are created by repetitive, directed conscious choice; that illnesses are brought into being by those same emotions, the energy patterns we have created as a distortion of that which God intended them to be. And thus it is no wonder that the personality structure of a girl with such a severe disability of the body would be replete with disturbances of a glandular-emotional nature. And her choosing was not always in a constructive direction despite Cayce's admonitions. This fact is evident in following the story through the events and the readings given her.

It was just a month after the last instruction and warning that Ginny received her twelfth reading. The hip was finally in place. She was ready to leave the hospital. The major therapy had been accomplished. She was undoubtedly feeling triumphant in many ways, and certainly those working with her must have felt a deep satisfaction in seeing a hopeless cripple come to active life once again. In his sleeping state Cayce saw that there was need, however, of caution and care still to be exercised, and he incorporated into his reading those necessary precautions. At the same time he saw the tendency of the girl to fall back into ways and habits that were destructive in their action on the body. And, perhaps with a great deal of unconscious patience, forgiveness, and understanding, he pointed out how the body would react if Ginny did not make certain changes of direction. It is interesting to compare his "refuses from the kidneys—causing blocking in the system" with the events that actually occurred ten years later—Ginny's death from acute dropsy which apparently developed following pneumonia. This is Cayce's comment:

> In the general condition of the body, we find there are *still* some of those conditions along the bone, where there is still some irritation. This ye should be mindful of, and the proper precautions taken as respecting this—or else we *will* have rheumatic conditions returning in the system, or either the return to those of the refuses from the kidneys—causing blocking in the system, or of other characters of poisoning; . . . but the moral and mental body *must* be in accord with that that has been attempted to be carried out, or to relieve it—or it had best not have been relieved. (409-12)

Ginny continued to make slow progress while at home, coming to the hospital for treatments. As the readings continued and the care progressed, other comments—almost unnoticed in their obscurity—were offered in the readings which strengthened the concept that Ginny's case was as any illness: an adventure in this dimension for a spiritual being who must at some time choose to obey God's laws and experience God's love. She found it difficult, but the theme in the readings was consistent:

As has been given, there is much to be accomplished in the mental attitudes of the body, towards self and to things outside of itself, as is in the material application—and unless those who apply, and those who receive, gain some conception of that being accomplished in a physical body, they are working very far wrong. (409-12)

Here Cayce gave the hint that, in all illnesses, there is a greater goal to be reached than simply the physical restoration. Attitudes, spiritual relationships, emotional expressions—all must be taken into account. For, as has been proven in a variety of ways throughout man's history on the earth: that which one sows, he must reap. And certainly, if love is a factor in the relationship between man and God, then a directional change upward (of attitudes and emotions) made by one's own choice will bring about a response in the body that changes the outcome. This is called grace, but it is a physical result as well as a spiritual one.

Ginny was reminded in her next reading that "much is given; much is required." Responsibility is assumed when one accepts in this manner.

What really does go on inside a person? How much does that activity of mind, memory, emotion, attitudes, belief affect the outcome of a physical ailment? We would suspect from this case of a very unusual young lady that the answer is "much." The specifics will remain unknown, certainly, and we have only hints to give us understanding and help—if Cayce's readings are to be of assistance in the healing of the sick in this world of ours. But we are given to understand that the body, mind, and spirit are truly one. And we take from this story the concept that the healing of an illness is intended to be a healing experience for the whole man in time, in space, and in patience.

No Surgery For Ken!

by Mary Ellen Carter

"Which side," Kenneth Ives began, with a troubled look on his face, "is one's appendix?"

"Why, I get mixed up on that, myself," said Doris, his wife. She put down the dress she had been hemming and glanced at him sharply. "It's your right side. Why?"

Kenneth, a young man of 24, moved slowly across the living room. "I've been having these pains in my right side lately. I feel kind of loggish."

Doris frowned. "You'd better lie down. Don't go to work tomorrow."

"Got to. We're having a lot of lawnmowers and bikes to repair these days."

When he came home from work the next evening, he felt no better. The pain had persisted, and he had broken out in a rash. He was experiencing dizzy spells, and a vein in his leg had become swollen.

As he lay morosely on the sofa while Doris prepared dinner, they heard a step on the front porch. "Yoo-hoo,

Discover the wealth of information in the Edgar Cayce readings

	ESP	Astrology
	Dreams	Atlantis
	Soul Mates	Psychic
Earth Changes	Karma	Numerology
Universal Laws	Reincarnation	Mysticism
Meditation	Akashic Records	Spiritual Healing
Holistic Health	Death and Dying	And other topics

Membership Benefits You Receive Each Month

- Magazine
- Home-study lessons
- Names of doctors and health care professionals in your area
- Library-by-mail
- Summer seminars
- Programs in your area
- Research projects
- Edgar Cayce medical readings on loan
- Notice of new Cayce-related books on all topics

Fill in and Mail This Card Today:

Yes, I want to know more about Edgar Cayce's *Association for Research & Enlightenment, Inc.* (A.R.E.®) (Check either or both boxes below.)

☐ Please send me more information.　　　　　　　　　　 | brc |
　　　　　　　　　　and/or
☐ Please send me a trial offer for membership.　　 | N31/PMZ |

Trial offer includes: magazine, free book, free research report, member packet. If at the end of 3 months' trial you wish to continue your membership, you need only pay the introductory membership level.

_____

Name (please print)

_____

Address

_____

City　　　　　　　State　　　　　　Zip

 Or Call Today 1-800-368-2727

You may cancel at any time and receive a full refund on all unmailed benefits.

**EDGAR CAYCE FOUNDATION and
A.R.E. LIBRARY/CONFERENCE CENTER**
Virginia Beach, Va.

OVER 50 YEARS OF SERVICE

BUSINESS REPLY CARD
First Class Permit No. 2456, Virginia Beach, Va.

POSTAGE WILL BE PAID BY

A.R.E.®
P.O. Box 595
Virginia Beach, VA 23451

785-71

**EDGAR CAYCE FOUNDATION and
A.R.E. LIBRARY/CONFERENCE CENTER**
Virginia Beach, Va.

OVER 50 YEARS OF SERVICE

BUSINESS REPLY CARD
First Class Permit No. 2456, Virginia Beach, Va.

POSTAGE WILL BE PAID BY

A.R.E.®
P.O. Box 595
Virginia Beach, VA 23451

785-71

**EDGAR CAYCE FOUNDATION and
A.R.E. LIBRARY/CONFERENCE CENTER**
Virginia Beach, Va.

OVER 50 YEARS OF SERVICE

BUSINESS REPLY CARD
First Class Permit No. 2456, Virginia Beach, Va.

POSTAGE WILL BE PAID BY

A.R.E.®
P.O. Box 595
Virginia Beach, VA 23451

785-71

anybody home?" It was Doris' mother, Matilda Derry, who had come over from her house across the street to bring them some of her preserves and to chat. "Not for supper. You go right ahead," she told them. "Why, what's wrong with Kenneth?"

"I'm worried about Ken. He's been having pains in his right side for the past several weeks. And they're getting worse!"

Kenneth groaned. "Chattering women!" he mumbled.

The pains became so severe that he could eat no food, the attacks of agonizing pain making him clutch his abdomen. As he started to bed at 8 o'clock, he suddenly doubled over, pain gripping him through the middle. He turned ashen and would have keeled over if Doris hadn't rushed to his side to support him.

Matilda went to the bedroom and turned down the covers. "That," she told Doris after they had gotten him gently into bed, "is a very sick boy."

Doris had grown up with Edgar Cayce's concepts of healing. She had heard her mother recount his successful cures many times to friends, had seen her sister cured of a long-standing illness, and she herself had been cured of an infection. Now, the two women exchanged glances.

"I think," said Matilda, "it's time to call Edgar Cayce."

Although Edgar Cayce generally gave only two scheduled readings a day, he was always willing to give one in an emergency. When Matilda had told him of the emergency for Kenneth Ives, he prepared to give a reading right away. It was given at 9 o'clock.

The disturbing conditions in Ken's body were of long standing, said the reading (1003-1), acute at present. "As we find, there are those conditions in the ascending colon that are in the form not only of an engorgement but in the way of producing—because of the position— toxic forces in the system."

The rash was due to the poisons being carried through

121

the superficial circulation. It alternated at times with spots in various parts of his body. The engorged veins were due to pressure in the coccyx area produced by a lumbar disorder. They were to be mindful at present of the inflammation in the caecum area, "though with the corrections of the pressure in these areas, and with the adjustments in the lumbar and coccyx area, these conditions should disappear."

Treatment should begin with painting the lower caecum area and that of the ascending colon with three parts laudanum to one part aconite. "Then apply the castor oil packs over same. This should be kept up continually for four or five hours. Then give a soda enema, a colonic—using the high colonic irrigation, as far as may be attained; not to cause too great a quantity at the time, but a tablespoonful of baking soda to each quart of water used."

After repeating all this the next day, Ken should have an osteopathic adjustment "in the lumbar, sacral, and coccyx areas, coordinating this with the 9th dorsal and solar plexus and the brachial plexus area. . . .

"Do not allow temperature to arise. If so, inflammation will have set in sufficiently to necessitate operative forces."

However, if the procedure was followed "with the diet consisting of fruit juices, a little beef juice—and keeping the body quiet, these should—without irritation—relieve these pressures in the body."

What had caused his dizziness and the swollen veins?

"Toxic forces and the pressure on the area to the liver," was the answer, "and the lack of the secretions of the gall duct and gall area."

After the third day of this treatment, Ken should have large quantities of olive oil, half a cupful. The adjustments should be taken once each day for three days and three more on subsequent days as needed.

"Is this condition what is known as appendicitis?"

Any inflammation [in that area] may be termed appendicitis. The condition in the present is *above* the appendix area, and may be seen or felt by the examination of the ascending colon—which lies between the lacteal ducts and the caecum on the right side, you see."

If the stoppage made for too great an inflammation, it would be necessary to take measures to prevent gangrene. "At the present, as we find, it is not indicated that the appendix is involved so much in the condition."

There was a practical nurse who happened to be present for this reading. Mrs. Jennie J. Jordan came to the Ives home and administered the treatment prescribed. She started with the laudanum and aconite solution on the lower caecum area. Doris helped with the castor oil packs and the soda water colonic, which was necessarily to be given under Mrs. Jordan's supervision. They repeated this routine the following day; by night time, Ken was out of pain and on the road to recovery!

He was, of course, very weak. Great care was taken that he didn't develop fever: he drank much beef juice and fruit juice. He slept and rested.

The next day, Kenneth began osteopathic adjustments by M. L. Richardson, D.O. Five days after his attack, he was back at work in the shop—a well man.

It is heartening to note that on September 14, 1964— 29 years later—Kenneth reported that he never resorted to surgery and that he never had further trouble in his appendix region.

Medical Commentary: Appendicitis

Appendicitis is still one of the most difficult diagnoses to make of all acute abdominal surgical conditions. The problem is solved if a surgical course is chosen; but when this is not the case, the problem of diagnosis often remains clouded.

Ken's predicament, then, despite the diagnosis of appendicitis which is carried in the Cayce readings index, will never be proved. He may have had a true case of acute appendicitis, or it may have been one of the other abdominal conditions which often fool the doctor prior to surgical intervention. His symptoms appeared rather typical.

Cayce himself, interestingly, never called the condition an inflammation of the appendix. He said that there was inflammation and engorgement of the tissues in the ascending colon, *above* the caecum and the appendix area, which, however, could get worse if proper care were not taken and could bring about a gangrenous appendicitis from an extension of the inflammation.

In the medical mind—at least the mind of the general practitioner, with which I am most familiar—a case of acute appendicitis is simply that. There is an irritated and swollen appendix, sometimes caused by a fecolith, sometimes by causes which we cannot discern. But when the appendix is removed, the person gets better. Apparently nothing else is wrong in the body, or, at least, that is what we think. When inflammation progresses to the state of a gangrenous appendicitis with pus formation, we still give little thought to what the events were that perhaps led to the appendix becoming inflamed in the first place.

Cayce's evaluation of this particular man, with a long history of right lower quadrant trouble, who was having rather severe abdominal pain—a typical story of recurrent low grade appendiceal inflammation—is interesting in its complexity of physiological malfunction.

Let us suppose that Cayce was thorough and correctly clairvoyant in his evaluation of this man, as he apparently was in *so many* of the 9,000 times that he gave physical readings in illness of the human body. The picture that we get, then, has many ramifications.

In this reading, he does not state the relationship of the appendix to the other lymphoid structures, but in other instances, he does go to great lengths to discuss the lymphatic system. He relates it very intimately to the nervous system, in a way that is not recognized in the anatomy-physiology texts. He puts the appendix and the tonsils in the same family, never recommending the removal of either of the structures unless disease had progressed beyond the ability of normal treatment procedures to restore them reasonably. He relates all lymphoid structures—including the Peyers Patches of the small intestine—to the thymus gland and the emotional-hormonal-neurological impact of that gland on the life of its owner.

125

In the Cayce readings, the thymus is also known as one of the seven spiritual centers of the body, and is called the heart center. Psychics see vortices of energy in all areas where the spiritual centers are located, and the thymus is no exception. Thus, if there is anything at all to the psychic perceptions Cayce and a host of other people throughout the ages have demonstrated and talked about, then the appendix, as part of the lymphatic system, has a spiritual as well as a physical reality and implication. Interesting thought, isn't it?

In the intricate relationship of functions which create a normally active and healthy body, Cayce saw a group of problems existing which contributed individually toward the development of the symptoms which Ken brought to the psychic for evaluation.

In discussing this problem Cayce talked in terms of systemic malfunctions, old-fashioned (but meaningful) terms, common sense, and osteopathic concepts. He saw a condition existing in the body which, had it undergone surgery at that time, might have revealed to the surgeon a retrocaecal appendix, perhaps hung up a bit high in its retroperitoneal location, with perhaps the ascending colon ptosed a bit, or disfigured from its normal location. This is not too uncommon a finding and is most distressful to the preoperative diagnostician. The appendix at the point of surgery would not have been inflamed but would have been recognized as a potential source of real trouble.

But Cayce saw many things going on as he surveyed the situation with his psychic eye. They all contributed to or were involved in the process.

1. "Disturbances in the eliminations of the body." This would mean, I suppose, that constipation had existed in varying degrees for a long time; that perhaps the kidneys were not eliminating as they should. It may have meant for Ken that his poor diet had suppressed the function of the lymphatic

system itself, which is the beginning of the eliminations at the cellular level.

2. Circulatory conditions resulting from the poor eliminations were set into motion and prepared the way for further trouble.

3. Engorgement of the vessels and the tissues of the ascending colon developed into inflammation of the area and a degree of systemic toxemia affecting the entire body.

4. The superficial circulation carrying the toxins produced a tendency toward a rash, especially in the "emunctory" centers—the axilla, groin, knees, elbows, and neck.

5. The veins in the lower extremities became engorged as part of the circulatory disturbances and as a result of pressures (of an osteopathic nature) in the coccyx area. He indicated in an extension of his comments that lesions and subluxations in the coccyx, sacral, and lumbar parts of the spine were part of this man's primary problem.

6. Poisons brought about through the deviations from normal described above created then the pains and spasms and the acute syndrome, which was obviously called an appendicitis.

7. The circulating "drosses," as Cayce would call them, not only caused those conditions and problems listed above, but also created a toxic effect on the liver and a depression of function of the gall bladder.

The primary therapy needed to be directed toward the inflammation existing in the ascending colon because of its tendency to migrate toward the caecum and the appendix, which would then pose a serious problem.

Perhaps we as physicians cannot daily explore the details of the aberrant functions existing in the body as we survey a patient and try to decide what is wrong. However, I believe we will never understand the body until we understand and put into its proper place the function of the body as a whole, composed of its integral functions. Until we realize that the function of a part and not its structure is the essence of the life effect that it has, we are still walking in the dark.

Cayce's evaluation, then, may be more than a psychic observation of what is wrong: it may be a word picture of where the action really is.

Then, given a condition that was called appendicitis by those around the patient, and described as a group of failing functions by a sleeping psychic, let us follow the suggestions for the relief of the problem and see what rationale was behind Cayce's recommendations.

Some of the most important suggestions in a given reading are often put in a cryptic manner, almost as an aside—almost as if he were saying: "Listen carefully if you want the full import of what is being said." It was in this manner that Cayce recommended rest for Ken for three days: "keeping the body quiet."

Throughout this material collected for a period of over forty years, however, much was said about rest. For any ailing body, rest is a primary factor and apparently has no substitute because of the need within the body for a balanced function of the autonomic nervous system. During rest and sleep, balance of the autonomic is, to a great extent, restored. If the body is contracting an illness of any sort, it is understood that something within the body has been put through stress by the progression of events, and rest is usually one of the necessities in changing the status quo.

I have never painted an area of the body with laudanum and aconite, in any combination. Nowadays the former is not available, even by prescription, while aconite is seldom used. Both are prepared as a tincture, laudanum being a tincture of opium. Aconite as a tincture produces a local sensory paralysis when applied. I would assume Cayce's recommendation to use this combination was based on its efficacy in such situations, since perhaps local anaesthesia on the skin might well produce a relaxation of afferent impulses from the corresponding autonomically-innervated internal organs. This is not too unusual a physiological response and would indeed relieve the spasm and pain which was Ken's primary concern at that moment.

Cayce then told the patient to have a castor oil pack (a folded-over piece of flannel cloth saturated with hot castor oil) placed over the abdomen for four or five hours. A piece of plastic was to be placed over that and then a cloth such as a towel to hold both into place. Cayce did not say whether or not to use a heating pad over the pack in this instance, though most of the time he recommended such a pack, it was used with heat.

Several years ago I did an exhaustive search of the medical literature back to 1911. I was looking for castor oil references in preparing a monograph[1] on the use of castor oil packs as Cayce had suggested they be used and as I used them in 81 different cases. This search revealed a very few, but quite interesting data.

Douglas W. Montgomery, M.D., wrote in 1918[2] of the oil which he described as coming from a beautiful plant with large palmate leaves, often called Palma Christi, the palm of Christ. Somewhat facetiously, I suspect, he said: "If as a child, I had known this sonorous name, it might have mitigated the misery I often suffered in having to take the oil. A very determined and energetic Scotch auntie regarded 'a crumb o' oil,' as she used to call it, as a universal remedy of exceeding potency in both moral and physical contingencies; and indeed, there is no doubt of its efficiency as a cleaner."

Montgomery's observations are undoubtedly of interest and relate to Ken's use of the castor oil packs. He observed that in diseases of the skin, the use of castor oil is

[1] William A. McGarey, *Edgar Cayce and the Palma Christi*, A.R.E. Press, Virginia Beach, Va.
[2] D. W. Montgomery, "Castor Oil," *J. Cutaneous Disease*, 36:466, 1918.

of importance inasmuch as a clean alimentary canal is conducive to a clean cutaneous surface. "It would appear that the medicine acts particularly on the ascending colon, and this is interesting, as it is undoubtedly a fact that many of the more active skin reactions are caused by poisons generated in the caput coli, a favorable location for the anaerobic proteolytic bacteria." He further pointed out that in the work of W. B. Cannon, in which castor oil was given to an animal with its food,[3] there was a serial sectioning of the food in the ascending colon followed each time by antiperistalsis which swept the food back—a type of action well fitted to clear out the haustra of the colon, "those pockets which in colonic sluggishness must tend to become especially dirty."

Schoch[4] later followed up on this information and noted some dramatic results in severe skin eruptions following the administration of often just a single dose of castor oil.

Ken took no castor oil by mouth, but he did have trouble with his ascending colon, certainly; there was a sluggishness and an engorgement of the tissues there, and his eliminations were not normal. My observations in the use of these packs revealed that abdominal administration of the pack often produced a cleansing reaction within the large intestine in a manner no one has yet been able to fully understand.

The packs may have started the elimination of the trouble in the ascending colon, which was then further retarded by the high enema given following the packs. Soda water used in the enema would aid in producing a more alkaline condition within the body which, in the case of acute infection, would bring about a more positive recuperative state of being, according to Cayce's reading.

[3] W. B. Cannon, *The Mechanical Factors of Digestion,* New York: Longmans, Green & Co., 1911, p. 151.
[4] A. G. Schoch, "The Treatment of Dermatoses of Intestinal Origin with Castor Oil and Sodium Ricinoleate," *So. Med. J.,* 32:326-328 (No. 3), 1939.

This need for an alkalinity was emphasized by Cayce's suggestion that Ken take only fruit juice and beef juice at first. The latter is prepared by placing raw beef in a glass container, loosely capped, then placing the glass in a pot filled with water which is allowed to simmer three to four hours. The fluid collected in the glass jar is then strained off and taken a tablespoonful at a time, bringing strength to the body without the assimilation of the meat which would then have to be eliminated.

The second day, after being relieved of the pain and spasm, Ken was again given castor oil packs and the enema containing a solution of soda. Following the enema, he was given an osteopathic treatment concentrated on the coccyx, sacrum, the ninth dorsal area, and the brachial plexus area of the spine. This, according to the readings, was to bring about a balance in the nervous systems of the body and relieve pressures which had existed there for a long time.

After the third day's regimen identical with the second, Ken was given another remedy, aimed at the inactive and sluggish liver–gall bladder complex of organs. He took a half cup of olive oil. This certainly must have been the hardest part of the therapy.

Thus, the eliminations, the circulation, the local inflammation, the toxemia, the rash, the liver and gall bladder toxicity, and the symptom complex were all dealt with in Cayce's suggested therapeutic course. The suggestions were followed, including a third osteopathic treatment on the fourth day, and Ken was back to work and apparently healthy, hale, and hearty.

An interesting case, and one which I find very logical and reasonable. If I were to venture an opinion as to what was the most important part of the entire therapy, I would vote for the castor oil packs. It seems to have had most to do with his recovery, the others being aids, perhaps, the packs being the primary therapy. However, that's like diagnosing an appendicitis *after* surgical removal. The challenge, the question, is not there.

Teenage Arthritic

by Mary Ellen Carter

Under a large maple tree that shielded her from the heat of the July sun, eighteen-year-old Sarah Blanding sat on a blanket and watched an ant lumber briskly over the mountainous folds. *I'll bet if your knee hurt, you wouldn't be traveling so fast!* she thought.

She heard the back screen door slam and the familiar step of her father. "There's my princess!" he called to her.

He took a lawn chair in the shade and accepted the glass of iced tea she offered him from a pitcher. He gave her a fond look. "How's the knee?"

Sarah adjusted the heavy, wet pack on her leg. "Dr. Frank told me to use hot salt packs. But I've been applying them for a week, now, and I'm actually worse!"

"Maybe we should try some other doctor."

"Oh, maybe. Then I'll beat you at a game of tennis, when I'm well."

"You'll have to look sharper than *that!*"

Sarah squirmed and grew pink, conscious of an eczema on her face and neck which had plagued her for years. Her father's idle remark had somehow touched off her sensitivity about it.

He seemed not to notice but said with belated tact, "You *are* looking brown and pretty these days. But maybe we'd better call the doctor about your contrary disposition."

"Daddy!"

As the days wore on, the pain in her knee was compounded by new aches in joints throughout her body. Now unable to bend her knees, she found she could hardly walk. At night she found the pain kept her from sleep.

In August she tried a series of diathermy treatments, but after these, she later testified, "I had eight afflicted joints instead of the six I had when I started."

Specialists x-rayed and examined her thoroughly, only to advise her that she had arthritis from some unknown source. Medicine they prescribed failed to help. "The only thing I think might help at all," said the specialist in charge of her case, "is that you go to Arizona to live."

When Sarah and her mother told Hal Blanding this, he said, "Well, if it will mean that Sarah can get well, then we'll move to Arizona!"

John Tydings, a real estate salesman, sat in their living room and talked about property values. With heavy hearts Ruth and Hal had shown him around. He had peered into corners, inspected the furnace. Sarah sat in her chair, a pale little bundle of aches and pains.

"Would you mind telling me why you're moving?" asked the salesman.

"Not at all," Hal replied. "Our daughter here is ill with arthritis. We're hoping the climate in Arizona will help her."

"Hm." John Tydings looked at Sarah with interest. "Mighty young to be having arthritis, aren't you?" He paused. "I hope you don't mind my being so personal, Miss Blanding. But it has occurred to me there might be someone who can help you . . . Of course, if he does, you might not want to move to Arizona, and then I'd have to let you folks keep your house . . ." He ended with a soft laugh.

Hal looked at the salesman curiously. "Just what do you mean? Who is this person?"

"His name's Edgar Cayce—a fellow who lives in Virginia Beach and gives diagnoses and treatment like a regular doctor, for people doctors can't help. He helped me and others I know."

It was October 15, 1932. Sarah herself wrote to Edgar Cayce: "My trouble is in my joints. Doctors have told me it is arthritis . . . I have considerable pain in all my joints, and am subject to severe night sweats."

Her reading was taken on the twenty-first. A few days later, her mother handed her a large envelope addressed to her. Sarah tremblingly opened it and read. It took a while, for the reading was three pages long, single-spaced typing. Ruth, growing impatient, said, "Well, what does it say, dear?"

Lying on the sofa, Sarah looked up with a smile. "It says a lot about diet."

"Is *that* all!

"Not quite. It says I have to take something called Atomidine. Later, I have to have epsom salts baths."

"Why, that's simple."

When her father came home from work that evening, Sarah gave the reading aloud to her parents: "We have the body here, Sarah Blanding. Now, as we find, there are abnormal conditions in the physical functioning of this body. These conditions, as we find, would prove very interesting and worth while in considering a condition that in many portions of the country, and in all portions to some extent, is gradually becoming on the increase, and that has proven most unusually hard to cope with: for conditions are so often hidden that it is hard to find the source or the cause of that the professions have called 'the point of infection.'

"Were the pathological conditions studied in the proper light, taking some that may be given here as the basis for investigations, we find that this case would prove very helpful and beneficial in many other similar conditions; for in this body the point of infection is hidden, yet in the basic forces of the metabolism and katabolism of the system may it be located, as the lack of elements necessary for the developing of that which makes for the regeneration in the elemental forces of the living organism to function balancedly for the proper coordination and physical balance throughout the system.

"First, in the inception of this body, some nineteen years ago,—not what may be termed properly (as in old considerations) prenatal conditions, but as of prenatal *surroundings*—there were those elements taken by the body upon whom *this* body was dependent for that from which it drew its sustenance in the foetus or foetal forces of its inception. These made for first tendencies.

"Then, with the character of the surroundings of the body, the character of the water as assimilated, the general dispositions that made for the resuscitating forces in the assimilating system, in many portions of the body the glands have been deficient in some respects and overactive in others in supplying the elements necessary for the proper distribution of forces in the system.

"These are the points of infections, then, that make for tendencies in the structural portions of the body to become more active than other portions; not to the point where that the growth is turned into that position or manner where the elongation of bone itself begins, but rather the crystallization in the muscular forces and tendons, so that the substance is lacking that should supply to the joints of the extremities that oil or that plasm in its activity about same to keep the functioning in a normal manner. Were this turned, as it were, in one more infectious point, then we would have rather the tendency of

135

Elephantiasis Proboscidis in its inception; but as it is turned in the present—from those glands of first the lacteals in assimilation, from the activities from the spleen and those glands from the kidneys overactive, or the endrenal [adrenal?] and those in the lyden [Leydig] and those of the pancrean supplying, or carrying, or taking, or adding to the blood stream those forces that are as the chrysalis of the infectious forces from the adrenals—it makes for the stoppage, rather than the drainage from extremities, which must eventually turn into bone itself and become either Sleeping Paralysis or Stony Paralysis, or that more of the orthopedic nature that makes for a twisting and turning of the bones themselves, by the muscular forces becoming hardened into such conditions.

"Then, to meet the needs of such conditions, various stages of this particular disorder necessarily indicate that a different amount of elements are lacking or are excessive in portions of the functioning body; but in this particular body, at this particular period of the development:

"We would first be very mindful of the diet. Keep away from all forces that supply an over abundance of salines, limes, or silicon, or the like, in the system. Supply an overabundant amount of those foods that carry iron, iodine, and phosphorous in the system, for these will act against that already supplied to burn or destroy those tendencies of debarkation or demarcation in the activities of the glands. We would outline something as of this nature:

"One meal each day we would supply principally of citrus fruits, or nature's sugars, nature's laxatives in citrus fruits, figs, prunes, berries of most nature—any of the active principles in such; a great deal of those forces that may be found in the pie-plant, or the like; salsify, gooseberries in any of their preparations—whether those that are preserved or otherwise, provided they are without any of the preservatives; currants and their derivatives

136

(that is, properties that are made from them, you see, *without pre*servatives); pomegranates and their derivatives; pears and their derivatives. Beware of apples and bananas among the fruits. Beware of any that would carry more of those that would add silicon in the system. One meal each day would consist of foods selected from such as these.

"Then there should be one meal almost entirely of nuts, and the oils of nuts; so that the activities from these in the system are such as to produce a different character of fermentation with the gastric forces of the stomach and the duodenum itself; so that the type of the lactics that are formed in the assimilation become entirely changed, so that the hydrochlorics that are formed in the system— or that are necessary to supply to the non-acid forces as they enter the system, or acid that make for turning of the system that which will gradually build in the pancreas, the spleen, the kidneys, the duodenum, those various folds themselves, more of those forces that will lessen the tendency for the accumulation of those conditions in extremities, where carried by the circulation itself.

"The evening meal may be of well balanced vegetables that are of the leafy nature, and that carry more of those properties as given. We will find much in turnips, eggplant (no cabbage of any nature, either cold or cooked), some characters of beans—provided they are well dried and grown in a soil that is different from that carrying iron, see? These will aid. The meats should be preferably (when taken at all) of wild game or fish, or oysters, or sea food.

"So much for the diet!

"Then we would take also, internally, those properties of Atomidine. This is iodine in a form that it may be assimilated in the system. In the beginning, if this is taken in large quantities, it would tend to make for a greater stiffness. Then, we would begin with small quantities. Twice a day take three minims in water, morning and evening. Each day increase the amount one minim, until there is being taken at least ten minims twice a day; then stop for five days, then begin over again.

"At the end of the third period of taking the Atomidine, we would begin with epsom salts baths (not until the third period of taking the iodine, see, or the Atomidine—which is iodine). These would be taken once a week; add five to eight pounds of the salts to sufficient water in the bath tub to cover the body up to the neck—which would be five to eight pounds to twenty or twenty-five gallons of water. The water should be just as hot as the body can well stand; as it cools add more hot water—and the body should lie in this for at least twenty-five to thirty minutes.

"After coming from this bath, the body should be rinsed off in plain water, then rubbed down thoroughly; massaging thoroughly into the whole of the body (that is, all of the cerebrospinal, all of the shoulder, head, neck, ribs, arms, lower limbs, toes, feet, hands, fingers) a solution of equal parts of olive oil, tincture of myrrh and Russian White Oil. Heat the olive oil first, then add the same amount of tincture of myrrh while the olive oil is hot, and while cooling stir in an equal amount of the Russian White Oil—and this doesn't mean any of those that are of the paraffin base, but rather that which has been *purified*, see? This should be massaged in thoroughly, all that the body will absorb. Following this (Because it will make the body rather oily), a general rub off or sponge off with rub alcohol. After such treatments, of course, the body should rest.

"When this has been taken for a period of three to five weeks, then we will give further instructions. Remember, the diet must be kept up; remember, the Atomidine must be kept up for this full period, and then further instructions would be given.

"Ready for questions.

"Q.-1 What causes severe night sweats, and what may be done to correct it?

"A-1. We have given what may be done, and we have

given the cause; for with these conditions that are caused by the glands' functioning, and the attempts of the system to reject these conditions, it would make sweat break out on anyone!

"Do as we have outlined, and then when the period has passed as given, we will give further instructions.

"We are through for the present."

The Blandings listened in wonder, and Hal said, "Let's not waste any time!"

Taking a personal interest as always, Edgar Cayce wrote Sarah a few days later: "The information gotten at your appointment was mailed to you some days ago. I feel that I should write and insist that if possible you make a sincere attempt to carry out the suggestions given. From what you have said, and the reading, I feel that the medical profession has offered little or no hope for any permanent relief. If you can get the whole-hearted cooperation of a friend or nurse, there should be no necessity for your going to a medical man at all. I believe you will be able to see the results from carrying out these suggestions. As indicated, there may be one period in taking the first properties when you will feel even worse than you have heretofore, a little more stiff and sore, but this will be your first reaction from the Atomidine. Your druggist will be able to obtain the Atomidine from the address given, if he does not have it already in stock.

"I would like very much to hear from you, and to know just how you get along . . . Please understand that it is our whole desire to be of service. Sincerely, Edgar Cayce."

As soon as they had obtained the Atomidine—they were able to find it at the local drug store—Sarah began taking the prescribed dosage. Ruth made sure that her diet was changed to the letter to consist of the fruits recommended, nuts, and leafy vegetables. It was severely restricted fare for a teenager, but as Sarah staunchly abided by the strange regimen, she began almost at once to benefit.

"On the morning of the third day," she was to write afterward, "I awoke and could actually bend one knee!"

She added, "Our happiness knew no bounds, we were practically delirious with happiness."

It should be noted here that her improvement began even before the entire treatment had been in effect. Only diet and Atomidine had been introduced; the hot epsom salts baths were not yet scheduled for another month.

On November 1, Ruth Blanding wrote to Edgar Cayce: "We are following your advice. It seems too soon to say or think Sarah is better but she seems to be. The pain in her knees is gone, they are some stiff. Her elbows are better (not so painful). There is color creeping into her face. She has been so white. She has had one spell of palpitation of the heart, and a night sweat last night (one night in 3 or 4 or 5) as before it was every night. She is we believe permanently better. She was not clear down but close to it, some days. Of course we are happy beyond words. We feel she is going to get well. We will be glad to let you know how she is from time to time."

After resting for five days, as she was told, Sarah began her second series of drops and when she had ended this series, the pain and stiffness were gone throughout her body, except for her left elbow, according to her mother. Sometimes she had pain in her hands. The night sweats became less frequent, and her eczema cleared up about the first of December. Her heart palpitation, for which she had taken strychnine under her former doctors, was now better.

Edgar Cayce replied to Ruth's letter asking about foods with lime in them, and which were to be avoided. ". . . I certainly hope and believe that as she begins with the baths there will not be the recurrence of the distress in extremities. Too, I feel you will see a great difference in other ways. Some may be inclined to feel that such baths tend to reduce the body, but I do not think you will find this the case; that is, it has not been our experience that such baths—when followed according to instructions through the readings—have materially reduced the weight, and they have been most beneficial.

"I think you might be interested in how the Atomidine . . . originated. Many years ago the readings indicated that iodine would be very beneficial to the system if the poison could be taken out of it. Information was given to several individuals as to how kelp (from which iodine is obtained) might be treated to make iodine non-poisonous. It was rather an expensive process, and the lack of faith on the part of the individuals prevented them from undertaking it. Only a few years ago a scientist working on the same proposition succeeded in preparing the product, which he called Atomidine. We know this man personally (Dr. Sunker A. Bisey). Many interested in the product feel it is good for practically everything, but the readings do not bear this out; however, wherever Atomidine has been used according to directions given in the readings it has been found to be most valuable.

"While the lime content of milk is quite high, the character of lime is quite different from that found in some vegetables, and many of the minerals that come from vegetables and fruits. It may be that if milk is to be part of the diet the pasteurized would be better, as it has less of the lime content; but to be sure, this again would have the tendency to produce constipation. Potato soup (which Sarah had found palatable) or the pieplant would not have that tendency, though you know—as a starch—potatoes carry a great deal of lime, especially potatoes that would be grown in Ohio. I do not think the sweetening of the pieplant would be detrimental, provided you are able to use beet sugar rather than the cane sugar.

"Thank you very much for letting us hear from you. I hope you will continue to write us every few days. Know that we are thinking of you and remembering you and Sarah in our prayers each day. . . ."

141

Contrary to expectations, Sarah's reaction to the first two epsom salts baths was more pain, lumps in her fingers, and a particularly severe night sweat. "The second bath was this past Tuesday night. Wednesday she ached all over and had a headache, her left thumb is still persisting (to be sore) and Wednesday was more acute, hurting into her hand and arm. Her right knee felt queer, rather creepy, like when she first took this . . .

"Her face and neck broke out badly this week even before the bath (per usual) about once a month and her period time came along Thursday; thus perhaps accounting for the aching on Wednesday. This is accompanied each time, it seems, with acute gas pains.

". . . her flesh seems flabby. We can feel a bump or lump along the right shin about two inches wide and three long. There are small lumps close against this shin bone at this spot. They are not sore . . ."

But several days after Christmas, Ruth reported: "We are glad to say at once this letter has a different message from the last one. Sarah's third bath was on last Tuesday and since Thursday her pain is all gone . . . She has stood the Holiday season very well. She has had a lot of extra work, trips up town for me as I was not so good myself. She is some tired, but no more than a well person would be."

Sarah continued to do "all the housework, cooking, and caring for" Ruth in January, evidently a time when Ruth herself became ill. Sarah steadily became better, although she had pain in her joints, which she was able to dispel with doses of Atomidine. She still had hard, sore lumps in her fingers and scaly spots on her face and neck.

A second reading given on January 20, 1933, found her much improved but full of encouragement to keep the diet and, when necessary, to take Atomidine and the baths. He still had much to say about diet. "As much of sea foods as convenient will work *with* the balancing of the forces in system, for they create a character of element in the minutia, and supply to the blood and nerve forces of the system, to the active forces in the principles of the blood supply and the functioning organs, an assimilated character of force that works with the activities of the body. Also green vegetables; as lettuce, celery, spinach, mustard greens, and the like. Also those foods that carry sufficient elements of gold and phosphorous, which are found partially from sea food and partially from the characterization of vegetable forces—as in carrots, the oyster plant . . . Never any hog meat, very little of beef unless it is of the very lean (and the juices), but mutton and wild game—or the white meat of the fowl, or the like . . . provided they are not taken in excess for the system."

For a week to ten days, she should take olive oil in small amounts several times a day; rest for ten days, then begin again.

She should exercise in the open, but refrain from standing on her feet for long periods—especially before and after her menstrual periods.

The scaly, itching spots were due to impure circulation and would clear up from the internal changes taking place. This could be aided by use of the violet ray. A kernel at the base of her left ear was due to improper circulation and improper contribution of elements from various glands in the system. There was, said this reading, scarcely any organ in Sarah's system where there wasn't some kind of infection—"for the *natural* condition of the system is to involve all forces in the body." These infections would be eliminated if she followed the suggestions.

By July, 1934, two years after beginning treatment, Sarah had grown so well and strong that she was working as a playground instructress in the hot sun, said her mother, eighteen hours a week. "She has stood it very well and is looking fine."

"I seldom have even a touch of arthritis, but when I do, a dose of the medicine prescribed sets me on my feet

143

again," Sarah told Edgar Cayce in her testimonial letter of August 14, 1934.

"We will never be able to express our thanks to Mr. Cayce for curing me and saving me from so horrible a death, as the reading stated that I would gradually die of sleeping or stony paralysis.

"My sincere regards to you and yours, Mr. Cayce, and I am proud to sign my name to this testimonial of you and your marvelous work."

Medical Commentary: Arthritis

by William A. McGarey, M.D.

Arthritis is a disease which probably affects fifty million people[1] in the United States alone. Sarah—the 18-year-old girl in this story—had the type of arthritis which we call rheumatoid or atrophic arthritis. It is also called proliferative arthritis or arthritis deformans. This type of disease process is characterized by inflammatory changes in the synovial membranes of the joints and in the periarticular structures and by atrophy and rarification of the bones.[2,3]

In the early stages, there is a migratory swelling and stiffness of the joints often with a rather typical fusiform

[1] *Arthritis—The Basic Facts,* Arthritis Foundation, N.Y. 1970.
[2] R. Cecil, "Diseases of the Joints," *R. Cecil's Textbook of Medicine,* 5th edition, Philadelphia and London: W. B. Saunders & Co., 1942, pp. 1408-1435.
[3] W. D. Robinson, "Diseases of the Joints," *Cecil & Loebe Textbook of Medicine,* 12th edition, Philadelphia and London: W. B. Saunders & Co., 1967, pp. 1390-1420.

swelling of the proximal interphalangeal joints of the fingers. Later on there is deformity with ankylosis and frequently an ulner deviation of the fingers as a sign of this disease. Subcutaneous nodules are frequent in these patients, and usually the disease is found beginning in young people, more commonly the male than the female. There is present anemia, chronic emaciation, loss of calcium in the bone structures, and the patient is rather severely and chronically ill.

Little has really been accomplished in establishing the etiology of the disease or in providing the physician with adequate tools with which to restore the patient back to full health. It is such an enigma that the Arthritis Foundation states categorically that there is no cure for the disease, and the sufferer from the condition is retrained from seeking such.

Sarah and her experiences give considerable food for thought when one considers the simplicity of the approach Cayce suggested and the manner in which he saw the disease process coming into being.

Rheumatoid arthritis—in this instance, if Cayce was correct—came about not through an infectious organism or through any other similar process, but through a series of circumstances that put the body into a stress situation. This stress affected the abilities of the body to assimilate certain substances, and this in turn created glandular conditions over the entire body which were abnormal. The glands in turn became overactive in some respects, deficient in others, in supplying the elements necessary for the proper distribution of forces in the system.

Forces again! This seems to be such a recurrent theme in the Cayce readings. However, forces, vibrations, balances, and incoordinations are not current parts of the medical thinking processes. In Sarah we find the forces making for hardening or calcification in some areas *overactive,* the forces making for hardening in other areas *underactive*. Speaking strictly in terms of forces, this is a body just all goofed up.

In order to study etiology of atrophic arthritis, as Cayce suggested we might, we would necessarily have to adopt a different viewpoint relative to body-function and a different attitude toward what is disease. Here, in this case, disease again originates from within the body. Cayce's viewpoint on this is consistent. Even considering that the mother had an improper diet, Cayce points out in other instances how an entity chooses where he will be born. He picks his spot, so to speak, and thus fits himself even into the physical heredity which he has built in past lives. One may not agree with such a concept, but one must agree that Cayce is internally consistent in his readings. If he was correct, we have a lot to learn about diseases; and we also have a much more optimistic outlook relative to rheumatoid arthritis.

One of the truly leveling influences in these psychic readings is Cayce's unconscious recognition of the equality of all human beings in their nature as creatures designed in God's image. Degrees meant little to him in the unconscious state, and this spilled over a little into his conscious awareness.

He wrote to Sarah after the reading was given and encouraged her to follow the directions given her in the readings. He told her that if she got some good help at home, then "there should be no necessity for your going to a medical man at all." Now this sort of a comment might be ego-shattering if one took Cayce's words at face value and his own medical degree as the emblem of the source of all knowledge about the human body. But most physicians recognize that the mysteries of the human body and its function are truly beyond our present comprehension and that a spiritual being manifesting as a physical body must be a strange entity indeed. Our knowledge today is insufficient at best, and degrees give us most importantly the legal right to exercise in the active world that knowledge gained in our studies.

147

Cayce's comment about the lack of a need for medical assistance brings to my mind the story Dr. Kenneth Starz[4] told me about a young lady who had arthritis, not in the 1930's but in the 1960's, some 22 years after Cayce died. After seeking medical aid for five years, receiving a variety of pain medications, and being diagnosed as a rheumatoid arthritic with little hope of recovery, this 32-year-old woman found herself nearly incapacitated for normal living. Her left knee was locked in extension. She couldn't get in or out of a car without help. She could not get up from a chair without assistance. She found her outlook becoming more and more bleak and hopeless.

At this point she noticed a book in a five-and-dime store. It was Tom Sugrue's *There Is a River*, the story of Edgar Cayce's life. She resisted the urge to buy it, but the idea and fascination persisted. She came back later and did purchase the book and read it. In the back of the book a case of arthritis, probably rheumatoid, was discussed at length, as Cayce had prescribed for the afflicted person. The woman felt that the castor oil pack therapy described in the scleroderma readings might also apply to her stiff joints which seemed to her to be like "stone."

She decided she would apply the readings. After a struggle of several months, she succeeded in following the diet, which the readings said had to be begun first. She had always been overweight and compulsively ate sweets and starches which were hardly permitted at all in the diet. After she finally was on the diet, she took epsom salts baths once a week, massaged herself as recommended, took Atomidine in cycles of five days, and applied hot castor oil packs every other day. On and on she went. She achieved no real relief; but she persisted, week after week, month after month. Still no results.

The story told in Sugrue's book was so meaningful in this woman's life that she continued regularly, persist-

[4] Kenneth Starz, M.D., Personal communication, August, 1971.

ently, consistently for a full year without results. Finally, one morning she awoke, and her shoulder was no longer aching. This gave her renewed faith, if you want to call it that, and she continued her self-designed therapy program. Gradually, almost imperceptibly, her swelling subsided in all three joints, the knee became fully movable, and after two full years of treatments (and over a thousand pounds of epsom salts) only occasional aching still remained when the weather changed.

She still continued with the treatments. After three full years, she stopped. Her enlarged joints were normal, her swelling had disappeared, her activity was normal, and all her aches and pains were gone. No medication was needed at all.

It is humbling and inspiring to hear how a person on her own, with faith, persistence, and two Cayce readings helped her ailing body to re-establish more normal functions and a more health-giving coordination between the organs and systems of her body.

The woman in Dr. Starz' story exercised faith and persistence in following a course of physical therapy treatments which brought about changes in a physical body through physiological adjustments that are undoubtedly related to the mental-emotional-spiritual changes and activities in the whole person involved in the experience. This story is not unlike the one told by Mrs. Carter. The change in time and circumstance is interesting and makes us wonder, indeed, what is the arthritic process, and is it really incurable, as some would have us think?

For Leonore, "The Glory"

by Mary Ellen Carter

The small, red-haired girl with glasses sat herself down on the beautiful green velvet winged-back chair, being careful to place her candy bar on the arm. She watched intently as a chunk of mud from her left shoe fell to the rug.

Later, Harry Swann, who owned the chair, came home from work and sat down to read his paper. The smudges of chocolate caught his eye. "Who's been sitting here?" he wanted to know.

Leonore, his wife, came rushing in. "Little Cissy Duggan from next door. Why?"

"There's chocolate candy on the arm. See?"

"There is!" she peered about the chair. "And mud on the rug. Oh dear." Then she looked at her husband. "Cissy's such a cute little girl. I really don't mind."

"Kids are a lot of trouble."

Leonore sat down in her rocker, close to him. "That's one kind of trouble I could use!"

He reached over and took her hand. "I know. Four years of marriage with no children, and no prospects of any. I wish . . ."

". . . that you had married a woman who could have children?"

"Stop that! Of course not. I just hope that someday, we will. I'm only 26, you're 24. There's lots of time."

"I'm sorry. You're right. There's lots of time." Then, "But I'm going to see the doctor tomorrow."

After examining Leonore, Dr. Fromm told her, "I find no reason for your infertility."

"I'm easily tired out," she told him, "and I break out frequently on my face. Would that have anything to do with it?"

"Well, you *are* underweight."

"And I have these pains in my head, neck, and lower abdomen . . . have had them for some time."

The doctor had no answer for this, but said, "Your underweight and tiredness are related."

"What?"

He had to repeat the statement.

"Oh. I also can't hear very well any more. I have a roaring in my ears! It's dreadful!"

Well, perhaps she should consult Edgar Cayce. She had been living by his readings since childhood, guided by her mother's interest in his work. She had not always followed her more recent readings as faithfully as she might have, but she felt that a reading now might get her on the right track.

"If Edgar Cayce can help me to get in shape to have a baby, I'll be happy," she told Harry.

On September 28, 1937, her sixth reading was given (578-6): "In some respects," it said, "we find conditions much improved and in others we find conditions have been retarded and are not as efficient as they should be in the reactions in the system. These particularly do we find in relationship to the pressures in the nerve sys-

151

tem and their reaction upon the sensory organism."

In the previous reading, Edgar Cayce had recommended adjustments in the upper dorsal and cervical areas, with corrections in the lumbar, sacral, and coccyx areas. "These pressures *now* produce upon the nerve system *greater* strains than has been indicated heretofore . . .

"Unless there is a change in the manipulations by the one administering same, we would change from that one . . . ; and have those corrections made as has been indicated. For not only will the removal of these pressures bring about a better normal condition, and a closer relationship between the emotions and the nerve system and the activity to the organs of the body, but we will find better assimilations, the body would put on more weight, the body would be hungrier, the body would not tire so easily, the body would not find the pains through the head and the neck and those through even the lower portions of the abdomen that become so severe at times.

"*We* would change then [from the present osteopath] to Crews' reactions [Gena Lowndes Crews, D.O.], the only doctor in that area who used the lymph pump.

"Make *specific* adjustments in the coccyx, *raising* the lower end of same. Coordinate this with the fourth lumbar. This *gradually* done. Then coordinate same, of course (each time coordinating all of these), with the upper adjustments in the 3rd and 4th dorsal, 3rd and 4th cervical, 1st and 2nd cervical and in the head and neck and the vagus center, but with these adjustments going *up* the spine!

"The next specific would be in the 8th and 9th dorsal segment, then coordinating these with the lower portions."

These were to be taken twice a week for two or three weeks, left off for two weeks, then taken again.

Asked about the deafness, he said that pressures in the coccyx area were not coordinating with those in the lumbar axis, deflecting from the ninth dorsal to the axis of the centers in the upper dorsal and cervical that make direct connection with her hearing. "Remove these pressures and these conditions will disappear!"

The breaking out on her face was due to poor lymph circulation from the areas where the nerve pressures in the upper dorsal area coordinated with her respiratory system. Hence, use of the lymph pump was recommended.

A blemish which had appeared on her left leg could be reduced to very little by rubbing castor oil on it for several weeks, daily; then, sweet oil.

Leonore had had an operation for removal of an ovarian cyst in January, 1936. When asked about this, Cayce said that this made for better conditions if the pressures were removed "so that there are still not those contractions during the periods of gestation for the activity of the organs of the pelvis."

"Just what can I do to make myself susceptible to pregnancy?" she asked.

"It will be necessary first that the pressures in those areas . . . be removed before there will be the ability for the organs to retain their activity at time of conception."

"Is there any special time for me to have this baby?"

"Not until these corrections are made and there is a building up of the bodily system itself. Then it would be beneficial." This would be possible by the following fall.

"Keep constructive in the thinking," he added. "Do not let *little* reactions produce animosities."

Leonore found F. C. Hudgins, Jr., D.O., to be a doctor who worked willingly with the readings. During the following six months, she followed through with Cayce's instructions, and on May 5, 1938, he filled out a questionnaire sent him by the Association. In this he confirmed that in his opinion, the patient's condition was described in the reading. He called her condition "Sterility, Dysmenorrhea."

The questionnaire asked: "Were the suggestions for treatment in your opinion proper for this condition?"

"Yes," Dr. Hudgins replied, "possibly could be added local manipulative treatment to uterus in order to correct malposition if present. Possible study to determine virility of husband."

"What results have you observed?"

"Patient still not pregnant—dymenorrhea cleared up, patient improved generally."

Another reading was given for Leonore, now 25, on October 18, 1938. This suggested for her specific exercises that would "make for a movement of the abdomen and the pelvis and the lower limbs." These, in addition to occasional manipulations, would now be sufficient to "attune" or "tone" her body. He said the exercises should be taken in the morning upon arising—the bicycle exercise in which she should lie down on her shoulders, making bicycle pedaling motions in the air with her legs.

Her condition was much improved, the treatments by Dr. Hudgins were "very good." She was still troubled by deafness. Cayce assured her that it was disappearing with the exercises and manipulations.

On December 2, 1938, she telephoned to Cayce the following questions: "1. Am I pregnant? If not, why don't I feel as I usually do near the period; and if so, what special precautions should I take to allow pregnancy to continue? How advanced is it?

"2. Would it be well to continue to wear the girdle for my back?

"3. Any further advice?"

Thus, at long last, the reading Leonore and Harry had hoped one day to be for them, began: "Yes, the glory of motherhood may be the part of the entity from the present experiences, if there is the care and precaution taken . . ."

Said this reading, osteopathic stimulation should be given to relax her tenseness but also to stimulate the retaining influences toward what may, without a disturbing force, become pregnancy. Such treatment should be given about once a week, "a quieting, through the manipulative forces" whenever there was too great an anxiety. Leonore should be careful not to get her feet damp or to take cold. She should keep wearing the girdle, which should be more an elastic for the abdomen.

"Has conception taken place?" she asked.

"As indicated, they may—it may not, dependent upon the conditions. The seed are present. The glory of such is present."

It had been one and one-half years since Leonore had begun treatment from Dr. Hudgins when he gave another report in answer to a second questionnaire. By now, he replied that results were "complete recovery." It was dated May 25, 1939.

The patient was now five or six months pregnant!

And on July 16, 1939, to Harry and Leonore was born a beautiful baby daughter.

Medical Commentary: Infertility

by William A. McGarey, M.D.

When pregnancy comes into the life of one who has previously been unable to have a child, it is a creative event that words cannot describe. The fact that children are born every moment of the day around the world does not lessen the miracle of new life to the individuals who had previously been denied the status of parenthood. The mystery of conception is most often pushed to the sidelines by the frequency of its occurrence, as if the simple statistics of the event explain how it happens. But for these two people, Leonore and Harry, the need to become mother and dad was a major factor in their lives, and they desperately wanted that miracle to happen.

In this story, it is not that Cayce was able to describe what Leonore needed to do to become pregnant that is to me the valuable data worthy of study. In our own private practices, Gladys and I, being man and wife, M.D.'s in general practice, have seen at least fifteen previously sterile marriages changed into parenthood situations by the simple administration of Vitamin E in one form or another. I am sure any physician working with sterility problems has seen the same thing happen through the use of nutrition, surgical means, physical clearing of the passages, hormones, or the simple process of adopting a child. A professor of mine and his wife gave up on having a child as they entered their forties—they adopted a child and within several months, she became pregnant. This is not an unusual story.

Suggestion, hypnosis, unconscious mind activities play a large part in the sterility problem and its solution. Fear of pregnancy has been shown to prevent conception at times, at other times to cause tubal implantation of the pregnancy or to cause spontaneous abortion. So many factors unnamed, as well as those I have mentioned, can alter the picture in the case of women who cannot get pregnant.

The valuable data in this story—it seems to me—are some of the physiological factors that Cayce suggests are involved in promoting the possibility and the continuation of pregnancy; the concept that the entire physical body needs to have a homeostasis that supports the possibility of conception; the idea that there is a "glory" associated with motherhood that relates the child and the parents with their spiritual origin and heritage. These data are worthy of study and of implementation in every case of man and woman who desire to become parents and in every physician who counsels and cares for the mother during pregnancy and often before conception occurs.

Cayce told Leonore in her first reading for this condition that she should not try to become pregnant yet—and in fact could not—until her body was more balanced and in proper condition to support the pregnancy. He told her that there were pressures in the spine which could be removed through osteopathic treatments and corrective manipulation. He also suggested that if the lymph pump therapy were used in conjunction with this, the results would be more certain and would come about more quickly. The patient did not take Cayce's recommendation wholly—she did not change doctors and did not get the lymph pump treatments from Dr. Crews as Cayce had suggested. It is interesting to note that whereas he had predicted she would have a child in the fall of 1938, under the circumstances of following his directions, she actually delivered in July, 1939.

The lymph pump is a manipulation of the chest which involves alternating pressures manually induced and which create an increased flow of the lymph through the chest cage—and probably, by extension, through other parts of the lymphatic system.

The actual problems of an osteopathic nature existing in Leonore's spine involved pressures and incoordinations in portions of the cervical, dorsal, lumbar, sacral, and coccygeal vertebrae, according to Cayce's insight. Relieving the patient of these conditions would have a profound effect on the body, physiologically speaking, if Cayce (as well as the osteopathic profession) is correct. A better functional relationship would come about between the emotions—or the endocrine system—and the entire nervous system; and the effect to the organs of the body would be enhanced as a result of this improved functional status. Cayce was implying, in other words, that the physical basis of emotions and thought—their proper relationship—would be bettered in all respects and the organs themselves would, as a result, function more normally.

With more normal liver, gall bladder, and pancreas activity, the assimilations of foods would be bettered; Leonore would put on more weight; her appetite would be improved because the utilization and metabolism of the food would be upgraded; her stamina and energy would be increased; and the symptoms of pains in the head, neck, and abdomen which had been so bothersome would disappear. "The removal of these pressures," as

Cayce put it, "will bring about a better normal condition."

The skin rash which Leonore was experiencing had its etiology, according to these readings, in poor lymph circulation from areas where nerve pressures in the upper dorsal area coordinate with the respiratory system. I assume this means that those areas of skin rash were deficient in lymphatic drainage because of lack of adequate nerve impulse from the centers which direct and control lymphatic activity. These centers are apparently associated very closely with the chest and respiratory system, which would be Cayce's reasoning behind suggesting the lymph pump treatment. This would have a direct or indirect effect on the lymphatic drainage of the skin itself. Most textbooks of physiology do not recognize autonomic control of lymphatic vessels, but this has been demonstrated anatomically in some lymph vessels of the abdominal cavity. Perhaps nerve supply has as much to do with repair and regeneration of the lymphatic vessels—perhaps more—than the flow of the lymph.

It has been shown[1] that hemorrhage frequently occurs in the subendocardial area soon after lymphatic flow is obstructed in the hearts of dogs. Cardiologists working with lymphatic problems such as these reason that areas of hemorrhage might lead to fibrosis when the lymph drainage is chronically inadequate. These findings could lead one to postulate that insufficient lymph drainage of any area could produce pathology—a dermatitis in the skin, for instance. Lymphatic structures of the body and their function are at the present time poorly understood in their significance to the health of the body. That they do act as eliminating channels of the body is understood, however, and when such a function is not up to par, disturbance in the nature of illness follows.

The deafness which the patient complained of had its

[1] "Lymphatics' Role Stressed in Cardiovascular Disease," *Medical World News,* Vol. 7, Jan. 21, 1966, pp. 100-101.

origin in the same pathology, apparently, that Cayce described as being part of the complex of pressures in the spine and spinal cord causing the other difficulties. It apparently did not need to be corrected in order that the body would be in good condition to bear a child, in the Cayce viewpoint, but Cayce did suggest that it would be better to clear it up once and for all. Leonore did improve, according to the records, but did not follow through on the directions given for this with consistency and persistence. Thus she was bothered with a recurrence and more acute loss of hearing later on.

When Leonore actually became pregnant, she was advised to have those things done which would *"stimulate* the *retaining* influences and the *development* of *all* influences *towards* what may—without a disturbing force—become pregnancy." This is a fascinating statement, for it recognizes that conception—the union of the sperm and the egg—has taken place; yet it implies that perhaps pregnancy—"being with child"—cannot be considered to be present until all forces of the body are proper to retain it: one might say, "until all systems are 'go'." Until, in fact, there is the proper homeostasis of the body.

At times Cayce apparently looked upon a situation with an ageless evaluation. Would the union of the sperm and the ovum produce that which would allow the woman to evaluate herself inwardly as a mother, carrying her child in her womb? Until the forces of the incoming entity, the physical condition of the uterus and its associated structures, the general condition and balance of the entire body physiology were coordinant in saying that this pregnancy would in fact be productive of a living child—then and then only did Cayce see an actual pregnancy, a mother with child. "This may—it may not. Dependent upon the conditions," Cayce said in his reading to the young woman. The seed of conception was present, but the possibility of fulfillment was still to be determined.

Perhaps Leonore's position as a prospective mother

can be better understood from the standpoint of the mind of Edgar Cayce if we were to look at a reading given for a 34-year-old woman (457-10) who was not yet pregnant but had been promised that she could become so. She asked many questions about preparing for pregnancy and motherhood and did, in fact, become a mother about a year later. Cayce's philosophy about motherhood shines through:

In giving information, or in answering questions respecting mental and spiritual attitudes, all of these should be approached from *this* basis of reasoning,—especially as preparations are made in body, mind and spirit for a soul's entrance into the material plane.

While as an individual entity, [457] presents the fact of a body, a mind, a soul,—it has been given as a promise, as an opportunity to man through coition, to furnish, to create a channel through which the Creator, God, may give to individuals the opportunity of seeing, experiencing His handiwork.

Thus the greater preparation that may be made, in earnest, in truth, in offering self as a channel, is first physical, then the mental attitude; knowing that God, the Creator, will supply that character, that nature may have its course in being and in bringing into material manifestation a soul. For, in being absent from a physical body a soul is in the presence of its Maker.

Then, know the attitude of mind of self, of the companion, in creating the opportunity; for it depends upon the state of attitude as to the nature, the character that may be brought into material experience.

Leave *then* the spiritual aspects to God. Prepare the mental and the physical body, according to the nature, the character of that soul being sought.

Isn't there, then, a challenge for Leonore and Harry,

161

and an opportunity for every practicing physician and for every prospective mother and father, in the implications suggested here, if indeed Cayce's work has a validity? Wouldn't it make a serious difference in a woman's life if she thought she were pregnant and received an admonition like this:

> The glory of motherhood may be the part of the entity from the present experiences, if there is the care and the precaution taken.

Maytime Malady

by Mary Ellen Carter

"Eleanor Belmont, I tell you, you have been taking terrible chances!" The short, little woman in a black straw hat settled herself on the rocker, her lined face wearing a dark look of disapproval. "At 74, you ought to have more sense!"

Eleanor passed a plate of little tea cakes and laughed. "Really, Glenda, you don't understand."

"I understand charlatan's work when I see it. Your daughter Joan has been completely taken in. I know she's sincere, so it must be that she's gone crazy!"

"Let me tell you the whole story, then say what you think."

Glenda shrugged. But there was a gleam of interest in her eyes.

"One morning back in 1926, just five years ago this past month of May, I started to walk out to my garden. The air was so sweet-smelling, up here in the mountains, that I felt I wanted to plant some seeds. Suddenly I jerked backward and collapsed in violent spasms on the steps. Joan rushed out to catch me, but I was stout then and she could hardly lift me."

"You're very thin now."

"Somehow she got me to the daybed in the back bedroom, and I lost consciousness, so I don't know just how . . ."

"Yes, I remember hearing about it. A convulsion, wasn't it?"

"That's right. When the doctor arrived, he examined me and found my heart was good, but he could find no cause for the spell. And I was so weak! Two years later, almost to the day, I had another. This left me even weaker. And in 1929—May, again—I had still another attack. Each time I would be weaker than the time before, for these convulsions lasted all day."

"How did you hear about this Cayce fellow?"

"Through friends of Joan's. This spring of 1931 I was feeling very bad again, so Joan decided to write to Edgar Cayce. She told him that I had been under the weather for some time and told him about my vomiting, pressure in my chest, pains in my arms. She asked him if I'd ever had gall bladder trouble, and about my diet, and if my heart was all right.

"The reading was taken on June 10. On that day, I remember, I was feeling pretty low but I tried to tidy up the house: if Mr. Cayce was to pay me a visit, I wanted everything looking nice . . ."

"If he was to . . . *what?*"

"Well, you see, while he's lying asleep there in Virginia Beach, he somehow comes to wherever you are to diagnose your case."

Glenda's eyes were full of alarm. "How can he do that, Eleanor?"

"Well, I don't *know,* exactly. Anyway, it was a warm, pretty day, and outside the mountains and the valley were still blue with mist. I dusted a bit around the living room. It's my favorite place . . ." and Eleanor indicated the time-browned photographs of her children and grandchildren on the wall over her roll-top desk. She had braided the rug herself, and she had tatted the doilies on the furniture.

"The time for the reading was set for 3:15 in the afternoon. I understood it was best to be in an attitude of prayer at the time of the reading. So I sat down at 3 o'clock. I felt at peace. I could look out over the valley far to the west where the mountains rise and fade into pale distances. I thought: *I will lift up mine eyes unto these hills, from whence cometh my strength.*"

"Did you feel or see anything unusual?"

Eleanor grew quiet. "Only a peaceful feeling."

Glenda was more impressed now than she cared to admit. "What was the reading like?"

"Well, it told me to do a number of things. I was to have castor oil packs for four or five days, and after that, to take olive oil in small doses, as much as I could take . . ."

"Castor oil packs! Hmf!"

"Yes, over my liver area. You use heavy flannel dipped in the castor oil and wrung out, and you apply them with hot salt packs. You keep them on for an hour or two each day."

"Go on."

"Then I took a high enema after several days of olive oil, then a cathartic made up from a prescription Mr. Cayce gave. I also took a pinch of elm in each glass of water I drank. I have to watch my diet—green vegetable salads at noon, fruit with rice or whole wheat bran cakes in the morning. Very little meat—only lean meat."

"What caused you to throw up?"

"My gall ducts not acting right." Eleanor smiled. "Edgar Cayce expressed better how I felt than I could. I can vouch for every line of that reading. Every bit is true. I'm following it to the letter."

"But, Eleanor, dear, how can you risk your life on the word of an untrained lay person?"

"Look at me!" Eleanor challenged.

"I have to admit," Glenda agreed, "you do look better than you did a few weeks ago." But she set her chin firmly and added, "But then, you would have gotten over your spell, anyway. You always do."

"Oh," Eleanor cried in exasperation. "Drink your lemonade."

Glenda ate her sixth little cake, put two more spoonsful of sugar in her lemonade, and winced.

"Why, what's the matter?" Eleanor asked concernedly.

"My arthritis again!"

On July 6, Eleanor's daughter, Joan, wrote to Edgar Cayce: ". . . Mother is giving your work the credit for her life. She feels like she would not be alive today except for the information and direction of the reading. She is improving every day and to say she is 'broadcasting' your work is expressing it mildly . . ."

To Joan, Eleanor said, "Keep track of the reading, and I'll follow the same course every year in the springtime."

The reading stated that "much might be given as respecting the history, or that as has brought about the disorders that at present exist." The condition must be "correlated *with* that which the body has *suffered* periodically in the past."

Pressure in the heart's action and a "heaviness" in the blood supply caused drosses in Eleanor's body, manifesting in pain in her shoulders, across both sides, under her arms, across the chest at times. Most of the heaviness around the heart was indigestion produced by functional and organic disorders in the eliminating system.

As the circulation attempted to be normal through the congested areas, "from poisons or accumulation in muscular tissue, as the intercostal, as in the brachial, as in the lumbar and locomotory plexuses of the system," even deep breathing at times gave catchy pains across her diaphragm.

At times, she had from the drosses acute use of her

senses and, at other times, "dimness of vision, drumming in the ears, fullness in the throat, and a general tendency of a throbbing feeling in the pulsations, or the capillary circulation."

Her pulse was low, with pressure high in blood supply. Her respiration varied from faster than normal to below normal. Her digestive system was, said Cayce, who used slang if it best expressed what he wanted, "all out of kelter!" There was gallstone accumulation which produced sour stomach, tendency for constipation, or else temporary diarrhea. There was too-frequent activity of the kidneys at times and only abnormal elimination through the pores, with swelling in her feet as reflex from the kidney conditions.

"To meet the needs," the first suggestion was the use of the castor oil packs over the liver area. These were to be kept for four to five days, followed by the olive oil doses, the high enema, and the cathartic. If the pinch of elm in each glass of drinking water became offensive, producing belching, she was to discontinue this and take instead yellow saffron tea, made with twenty grains to one pint of water, steeped, strained, and cooled.

Her diet was to be mainly liquid, with the fruits and vegetables predominating.

She was to use enemas when necessary to relieve pains from the pressure in the intestinal system. The last water used should be that carrying Glyco-Thymoline, or boracic acid as an antiseptic (in a gallon and a half of water, two tablespoonsful of Glyco).

A year later in 1932, during that fateful month of May, Joan reported to Edgar Cayce that: "Mother had spoken about having another reading but she has been talked to so much (folks trying to get her to save me from insanity) that I don't know what she now intends to do. But she seems perfectly well . . ."

Eleanor decided to have her check reading, anyway. Joan's letter explained: "My mother is not so well and

167

she asked me to write you for a reading, so give it at your very earliest date—simply write her the day and hour . . ." Questions asked were: "What causes breaking out with hives or itching bumps? Is the mineral oil now being used the right thing and should it be continued? Is she able to stand a trip soon to Virginia Beach?"

A few changes recommended now in Eleanor's check reading concerning diet and medicine brought about her continued gain in weight and strength. By early spring of 1934, Eleanor had been quite well for several years, but once more began to suffer some illness. She wanted another check reading.

"I owe the latter years of my life to the service Mr. Cayce has rendered me," she told Joan.

On the eleventh of April there was another reading. On the twentieth, Joan wrote: "When I wrote for the reading for Mother, I was very much disturbed about her condition. She had gotten so much worse. Her breathing was real laborious and panting, especially at night and when going up steps. She began at once on the new treatment and I can see a decided change already. While we were waiting for the reading our family physician chanced to come in here and, seeing how she was feeling, gave her an examination and told me that she had a leak, or I believe he said 'lesion' or something of the sort in her heart that was worth watching and to keep her absolutely quiet. Well, I was right much in hot water for I just did not know how the reading was going to sound to her, for she gets very blue and worried about her condition at times and I never tell her that I worried about her condition, but I knew I could not keep her from seeing the reading so you cannot know how relieved I was when the reading had no reference to a leak in her heart. In Feb. she had a pretty close shave with pneumonia and of course I was not surprised at a weakened heart condition. She still suffers with weakness, though her breathing is much easier. So I think she is responding very well considering her age. Where the reading says 'Many of the ministrations that have been outlined would be well to take or consider' etc. I had been wondering if that refers to the castor oil packs? If she keeps on feeling so weak I will try that again, for she received wonderful relief by it. Just at this time I have to be away and will not be able to give the vibrator treatment . . ."

Joan wrote once more on June 12 to say that "Mother was taken with one of her regular spring attacks on Apr. 25th and passed away on April 27th. I was not at home when she was first taken but hurried on as soon as I heard. She had not been able to react very well from the change in medicine, tho she was working faithfully and I believe had she been a little more careful of the diet it might have been different, I do not know; but if you remember the last rdg. was not at all encouraging, or not nearly so as the others. She had been gradually growing weaker all winter tho she made a brave fight . . . She said often the past few months that she owed the latter yrs. of her life to you."

In 1940 Joan stated: "The physician's analysis was heart weakness and gallstones. Her improvement was 100% when we followed the first rdg. I am sure that the Edgar Cayce treatment prolonged her life for 2 to 3 years."

Medical Commentary: Debilitation

by William A. McGarey, M.D.

When a woman has lived 74 years, she has experienced many things. Each experience undoubtedly contributes something to the quality of her physical health. Physical and psychological trauma, the ageing process, the residuals of previous illness, improper dietary habits, the stress and strain of life decisions—all of these contribute to illness in a multitude of ways.

Eleanor's difficulty was a problem in the field that today we call geriatrics. In the older patient, there is an accumulation of minor problems—sometimes of major ones—and the duty of the physician is to keep the geriatric patient as healthy, hale, and hearty as possible. I would suppose it is really our responsibility to help the older person to remain alive and vibrant and active until the change of environment that we call death comes about. It is a certainty that we can stem the tide only so long, then death must intervene.

Cayce gave several readings dealing with longevity. These comments would lead us to believe that length of life depends on a number of factors—one being how long one *believes* he can live, and another being how well one knows the laws of balance governing the physical body and how well he obeys them.

In the readings given this woman, a great variety of rather serious problems were identified, and one can almost sense Cayce's realization of the fact that a major rehabilitation was quite unlikely in this case. Actually, this is one type of evaluation done by every sensitive physician—the attempt to catch the degree of life potential present in a given patient and how much there is left to work with. Cayce "looked" psychically at her past history and said:

... much might be given as respecting the history, or that as has brought about the disorders that at present exist. These, as we give then, will be rather that as exists which must be correlated *with* that as the body has *suffered* periodically in the past. (356-1)

In other words, as he had mentioned earlier in the reading, there were numerous abnormal conditions in the physical functioning of the body, as well as organic disturbances, but here he was giving specific suggestions to relieve the episodic springtime convulsive syndrome. He was not at this point—or even later—attempting a full rehabilitative effort.

The question arises in most minds, as this material is studied, whether Cayce mimics the attitudes and procedures of a good physician or if some other explanation could be found for his basic excellent approaches in an unconscious state to the problems of the sick individual. It was exciting reading for me when I came across Cayce's own life reading that told about the time, many thousands of years ago, when, in a past life experience, he was himself a physician and apparently used these

171

same methods of rebuilding the body that we find described in the readings today. Undoubtedly a medical career in Persia 3000 years ago does not qualify a man for a medical degree today, but the soundness and basic quality of the advice given from this man with a probable Persian medical background certainly makes the material worth looking at.

And, at the same time, it gives one the feeling that perhaps the medical advice is based on more than information pulled out of a cosmic hat. Cayce had been there—according to his trance information—and he knew how to handle the tired, sick, often disgruntled patient. He knew how to keep a balance in the function of the body as he helped it to regain health. He knew the meaning of incoordination, and he knew the heartache that goes with the experience of illness in one's own body and in the life of a dear one. Because he had been a physician, he was aware of the sickness of the human body which needs relief.

With Eleanor, then, he gave suggestions that were designed to help out somewhat with the problem of cholelithiasis—the stones in her gall bladder had been bringing about much distress. The eliminations from the system needed to be improved in many ways. The intestinal tract needed soothing and balancing in its action. The nervous system was under stress and strain due to improper eliminations and the accumulation of normal waste products in the body musculature, the stress coming as the nervous system attempted to make the circulation of the body normal under these trying circumstances.

In readings given for epilepsy, Cayce suggested most consistently the use of castor oil packs over the abdomen and liver. These also were a regular therapy program for nearly all gall bladder problems. In view of the history of periodic convulsive episodes *and* gall stones with gall bladder irritation and congestion, it is no wonder that the castor oil packs were recommended here.

An electrically-driven vibrator was used along her

172

spinal column, to stimulate a better relationship and function between the cerebrospinal and the autonomic nervous systems. A diet designed to supply simple nourishment to her body was suggested. Elm water (or yellow saffron tea) to relieve the irritation within the intestinal tract and enemas to relieve pain and to act as a cleansing agent completed the first set of suggestions.

As these were carried out, Eleanor improved remarkably and apparently established a new basis of body balance which lasted the better part of three years.

This was good geriatric care, certainly. One wonders what would have happened if Eleanor had consulted a physician with Cayce's insight and could have been followed month by month. Would she have continued using some of these same rehabilitative measures to build an even more vigorous body, or would she have found such suggestions to be out of place in a doctor's office? Would she have paid less attention to her doctor than she did to an unconscious man who had a capability that has not yet been fully explained?

These questions cannot be answered, of course. It is quite apparent that the patient lived another three years, was greatly relieved for a period of time, and succumbed apparently to the same process that was going on when Cayce gave his first reading. All of which goes to substantiate a theory that illness *is* a process, probably set into motion by the thoughts, attitudes, emotions, and activities which a human being engenders throughout life; and it is most difficult to change 74 years' worth of patterns in a way that will bring about a major change in direction and thus a relief from the processes that create and shape the nature and activity of a disease.

As a physician, I would not like to be responsible for the results brought about in a patient I would see in my office only three times in three years. That is a tough proposition. Cayce was in this position. But perhaps in the thousands of years and several incarnations that had passed since Cayce had been a physician in Persia, he had grown a bit more patient, a bit more philosophical, a bit more insightful than he was in those days. This would temper one's outlook. And a realization of the concept that death also often brings real healing would make one's position in relationship to an older patient's physical-mental condition much more tenable, much more liveable, much more creative.

Call This A Miracle

by Mary Ellen Carter

Tony Castello was a skinny little six-year-old with large, dark eyes that held how many lifetimes of living and dying?

As his father, Ernesto, carried him up the steps of the Cayce Hospital, his mother followed close behind. "Don't be scared, Tony," she said. "Everything will be all right."

At the door there appeared a tall, lean man with a friendly, inclusive nod for the three of them. "Who have we here?" he greeted.

Puffing a little from the exertion of the climb with his burden, Ernesto replied with a smile, "We have my son, Tony Castello, Mr. Cayce . . . you are that man, aren't you?" He added, "You gave him a reading in March. It said he should be treated here."

"Oh, yes, we received your letter that you were coming. I hope we can be of help."

"Oh, Mr. Cayce, we have tried everything!" Rose Castello said plaintively. "Can you help him?"

"We will see," said Edgar Cayce.

Tony was admitted by Miss Gladys Davis, the pretty young secretary of Edgar Cayce, who smiled across her desk at the new little patient. His father gently put him down on one of the leather upholstered chairs in the lobby and gave a laugh of relief. Tony gurgled.

"You liked that climb, eh, Tony?" his father teased fondly.

"Especially the steps," Edgar Cayce rejoined.

The boy, anxious to join in the repartee, attempted to speak, but he could only jerk and writhe, his mouth opening wide, his head bobbing.

"He's really very intelligent," Rose hastened to explain. "He wants to talk. He likes you and he understands what you say."

"We've taken him to all kinds of doctors," Ernesto added. "All we can do is give him drugs. We try to help him walk every day, but it's no good. He still has to be carried everywhere."

"The doctors called this cerebral palsy, something that occurs at birth, isn't that right?" asked Cayce.

"That's right," Ernesto nodded. "But he's not retarded. We can tell he's learning a lot, he just can't make the physical movements to walk or talk. The doctors have said that all we can do is to train him to use whatever muscles and brains he has to function."

"What do they do for him?"

"There's nothing much they *can* do. We're supposed to get a walker to help him get around and to help him stand up." Ernesto sighed. "And there's muscle-relaxing drugs. But a lifetime of *that?*" And he gestured expressively.

The Castellos had obtained a reading for Tony on March 14, 1930. It told them that corrections could be made, that the results of treatment might prove "ideal." In many ways Tony was very special, the reading implied.

The derangements in his body might be brought to normal by means of proper adjustments. "This particular condition would be an interesting study from the structural, anatomical condition, if studied from the application of the radiograph and the reactions made with same," said this reading. The congenital nature of the condition had to do with the cerebrospinal system and those branches that lead from this to the locomotory centers.

"It will take patience, persistence, and some time," it continued, "but will be well worth the changes as may be wrought in the physical activities for this body."

Cayce then outlined a program of treatment: gentle manipulations, at first; use of the wet-cell battery carrying chloride of gold to the extremities and to the solar plexus; fresh air and sunshine that would "work wonders for the body;" body-building foods; and the use of the infra-red ray "to aid the bones' reaction in the system." (5568-1)

Changes would occur in ten days to two weeks after starting this program, but there would not be a permanent cure until there was the proper "rejuvenation" in the whole system.

The time required for a complete cure would depend upon how the body responded to treatment. A gentle approach would be needed in working with Tony. One should not use force but, instead, gain his confidence.

On the day following his admittance, Tony awoke in his room overlooking the ocean to see the panorama of long, rolling sand dunes and the wide sea itself. Treatments were begun with osteopathic manipulations, as recommended in the reading. These were done by Dr. Grace Berger.

"We're going to rig you up with a battery," Dr. Berger told him as she worked. "Then we're going to put a red light on you. That's called an infra-red ray. What do you think of that?"

Tony, lying still and obedient on the table, gurgled.

"We're going to do that every day: 30 minutes for the

battery and 20 minutes for the light. Then we're going to take you to the beach. Think you'll like that?"

Another gutteral sound from Tony.

"We'll give you sand baths and you'll swim in the ocean, every day." As she worked she moved his legs and arms and massaged his torso.

That afternoon, Dr. Lydic began the wet-cell battery treatment. This was used with chloride of gold in the solution, which was to be carried to Tony's hands, feet, and solar plexus.

The weather was still cool, so after a half-hour on the beach in the pale April sun, Tony was brought back to his room. He had a supper of broiled lamb, carrots and peas, and tomato aspic, with ice cream for dessert.

When Edgar Cayce looked in on him a little after bedtime, he saw a tiny, distorted form beneath the covers. In sleep Tony's face was tranquil. He was at peace in whatever dream world that he walked, straight and strong.

* * *

As the days passed Tony was given more time on the beach, where he was immersed in "sand baths" or put into shallow pools made by the sea, where he remained for short periods. He soon acquired a tan and began to gain weight. As Cayce had predicted, he was improving ten days to two weeks after beginning his stay there.

After three-and-one-half weeks, a third reading (5568-3) was given on April 28 recommending "good sweats," but that these would be torture if not handled properly. They were to be followed by rub-downs with equal parts of olive oil and tincture of myrrh, with special attention to the spine. He was to take small doses of quinine "to stir the liver and rid the blood of those *effects* of poisons by congestions." Care was to be taken against cold and congestion from too much exposure outdoors. With warm weather he was to reduce the infra-red ray to once a week, since he was able to be on the beach almost daily.

On June 10 a reading reported his progress as "very good." A more vigorous manipulation along the spine was given "to stimulate the nerve ends as they function through the muscular portion of the body."

In July, a reading stated that if the staff kept up the program, making for the relaxing of the muscular ends and the tissue forces in the extremities and radial centers of the cerebrospinal system, these would make for a "straight body, for an active physical force in same." Now Tony was to have a rub-down every evening with cocoa butter and olive oil alternatively; or, it might be with olive oil and myrrh, then cocoa butter.

The seventh and final reading was given September 1, when he was told he might go home. In the five months he had been there, he had "improved in many ways," as the reading stated. Gladys Davis Turner attests to his improvement for she recalls that he had gained, he seemed more alert, and certainly his color had returned.

"A cure of this kind takes time," she points out in reporting to me on this case.

The record states that at that time, Tony had a tendency to be overactive as his system responded to treatment and became stronger. At home he was to continue treatments which could be given through the radioactive appliance containing spirits of camphor. He was to have osteopathy once a week and oil manipulations to stimulate capillary circulation. He was to continue his building diet.

He left on September 3. In November his father gratefully wrote Edgar Cayce that Tony was still improving and "wishes to be remembered, and also his mother, to everyone they knew at the hospital."

On December 13 he again wrote to say that Tony was having his osteopathic treatments and that "he is improving all the time."

This case is not listed in the files as officially "cured."

No further reports were made on Tony's progress. Gladys Turner's efforts to get in touch with his parents were fruitless; more recent attempts on the part of this writer, 40 years later, were also negative.

However, the sleeping Cayce spoke so optimistically at the outset and in the final reading, regarding Tony's chances, that, knowing the *mind* of these readings, we are led to believe he recovered. Tony's marked improvement during eight-and-one-half months of treatment as suggested by Cayce was in itself a triumph. To Rose and Ernesto Castello, it was more than they had hoped.

Medical Commentary: Cerebral Palsy

by William A. McGarey, M.D.

Tony Castello presented a rather typical picture of what we call cerebral palsy when he arrived at the Cayce Hospital back in 1930. His type of problem, from the information available, seems to fall into the category of choreo-athetosis. About one-fifth of all cerebral palsy victims have an athetotic difficulty. That is, they display writhing and jerking movements of the body and face when they try to speak or accomplish any voluntary movement. Athetosis is one of the so-called extra-pyramidal cerebral palsies.

Cerebral palsy as defined is not a disease entity with a known cause or characteristic course but is rather a term of clinical convenience covering any impairment or impairments of neurologic functions due to brain injury dating from birth or early infancy. There are broad groupings of the problem which serve as well as any medical classification to distinguish the different types. Tony had the choreo-athetotic type. From the readings which Cayce gave him, the cause may have actually developed before birth.

Because of the difficulty in determining the cause of the problem, therapy has been at loose ends. Thus the aim of treatment at the present time is to help the child achieve his maximum potential rather than to become normal. Cayce takes a point of view in this particular case that such a therapeutic objective falls far short of the ideal. He implies that Tony could, in reality, get well, or at least normal enough to be considered well—able to control his body, his voice, his actions.

I am fascinated by Cayce's description of the problem this young man is given to deal with. He does not say it in so many words, but he points out that the difficulty stems from an improper distribution of nerves. The condition is congenital, he says, but able to be changed. The cerebrospinal nervous system is defective in that the nerves have, in a sense, sought out an incorrect distribution throughout the locomotory centers of the body. That is, those centers of the nervous system which are primarily responsible for receiving impulses from higher and from autonomic centers and relaying the coordinated impulses to the muscles in order that they will contract properly are, in this case, innervating the wrong tissues. It is a condition similar to a fouled-up telephone switchboard.

The nerves from the higher centers also appear to be involved in finding the improper distribution, the result being that when the child desires to say something, nerve impulses go everywhere except where they are intended. The individual must deal with a writhing, contorted mass of muscles and tissues that are undoubtedly utterly frustrating.

Cayce's answer to such a problem once again refers back to his recurring concept that man is a spiritual being with a mind that builds living as a material entity in a three-dimensional world. Sometimes man builds in the wrong direction, and he has destruction as the result. Cayce states that the body may be rejuvenated, it may

182

undergo constant rebuilding until it is normal. He implies that the nerve cells, given the proper impetus, may establish new channels, seeking out their proper distribution, and in the process bringing about a cure for the condition. The mind, he points out, works through the nervous system, and given the proper impetus, can re-map the pathways for the nerves, re-establish the proper connections with the muscles, and re-connect to the autonomic centers which bring about coordination to the entire body in its functioning.

Cayce, then, saw Tony as an individual who might be "with careful study, an *ideal* patient, an *ideal* result." (5568-1) He went on in the next reading to say that if "those suggestions be followed as have been outlined, in a consistent manner . . . *many* will call this a miracle." In other words, it is difficult to understand anything other than that cerebral palsy in this one patient could be cured—if Cayce was right.

It is indeed unfortunate that we do not have adequate follow-up data to see what did happen to this young boy. From my own experience in working with people with a difficult and chronic condition where little change can be seen in a short period of time, I would expect that the Castellos stopped working with Tony shortly after they got home. It is a bother to give massages or infrared lamp treatments or to use a wet-cell battery that must be applied in a certain way and must be refilled with water and other ingredients every month. It is discouraging. The only thing that keeps people going on such a program of therapy is a vision of what could be, a faith that such a cure can come about. The Castellos here had only Cayce's words. They did not have an understanding of the body, nor did they have the advantage of knowing that anyone else had ever successfully done this type of therapy for cerebral palsy. Many things were working against them.

This group of disadvantages calls to my mind the comment that Cayce made when they asked him how long it would be before Tony got well. He responded that it depends on the way and the manner in which the body responds. Does that mean that, in this case, Tony's will had a part to play? It probably means that if Tony were to rebel against the therapy, it would not work. Cayce also stated in the same reading that the speed of Tony's recovery would depend on how much confidence is built in him so that he does not feel forced in the application of his therapy.

However, there is no follow-up evaluation on this boy. Thus we cannot say whether the therapy would have been fully effective or not. In all of his readings, Cayce seemed to imply that the healing process, or the activity of regeneration or repair, involved not only the therapy that was given but the attitudes, emotions, and thoughts of the patient himself and those who were taking care of him. These factors, interposed into the picture, make the success of every therapy program dependent upon the individuals who are involved. Perhaps this factor applies more to the serious, chronic diseases but also, to a lesser extent, to everything that is treated in a doctor's office.

A little boy's bruise will heal quickly if his mother kisses it soon after the accident. A laceration will be restored to normal more efficiently if the person suffering the injury is not afraid and tense at the time of the suturing. The examples are virtually inexhaustible.

The actual series of treatments which were suggested in the seven readings given for this boy are all directed at a rehabilitative effort that Cayce calls regeneration and rebuilding. They were all aimed at the functions of the body, for Cayce assumed throughout his life that normalized and vital functions will bring about normal structures and a resultant full state of health.

Tony was told that the external applications of a therapeutic nature had to be coordinated with the internal. In this instance, the external were the massages with various oils (but particularly olive oil) which would act as food for the muscles and tissues of the extremities and for the tendons of the muscular apparatus. A patient of ours recently told us that, when she was a baby, she was vomiting so badly that no one could get any food into her body. In those days they did not have intravenous feeding. Her parents massaged olive oil over her entire body, using excessive amounts, and she responded and was able to survive on the food that the oil provided until she was able to take nourishment by mouth. So the idea of food or nourishment in this manner is not outlandish. We simply do not see it often and do not think of it as being a possibility.

The internal applications that Cayce had reference to were the wet-cell battery which was described somewhat in a previous chapter. Cayce visualized the vibrations of the gold chloride being carried into the body through the application of the low voltage battery which produces about 15 millivolts of electricity. The two leads were to be applied mainly to the abdomen and one of the extremities.

Gentle manipulations by an osteopath; sun, sand, and plenty of fresh air; infrared lamp treatments (especially when not out on the beach because of inclement weather); sweats, if properly handled; and 2½ to 3 grains of quinine for four or five doses "to stir the liver and *rid* the *blood* of those *effects* of poisons by congestion." These were other suggestions for therapy which Tony was supposed to be given in a consistent, patient, and persistent manner. The doctors and the parents were to keep a good rapport with him and work with him gently in a way to encourage his optimism and his trust. Diet was to be of a general building nature.

The massages, Cayce directed, along with the sun, sand, and open air would create within the systems of the body a building of the blood and tissue which needed regeneration. The massage would have further effect when done more vigorously in producing greater stimulation to nerve endings in the muscles of the body. When the olive oil and cocoa butter massages were alternated every other evening—that is, having one massage every night—it would make for better rest for his body and also for improved activity of the centers for autonomic coordination, which are located along the spinal cord. The massages would also improve his ability to be more active in walking and getting about.

Tony's problem is one experienced by thousands of people throughout the United States, perhaps by millions throughout the world. Cayce had something definitive to say about what was wrong inside the body, not too much about why or how the disease came into being. He commented at length on the possibilities of regeneration, at least in some cases, to the point where normalcy would be the design. If he proves to be an accurate prophet, our understanding of the body and its capabilities will undergo considerable change in the foreseeable future.

"For Life Itself Is A Service"

by Mary Ellen Carter

"Esther! Mrs. Goodbond's here to see us!"

"I wonder what for. Yes, I see the limousine has stopped out front."

Gordon Worth, 22, leaned forward on his cot by the window and nodded. "He's a new man, the driver." Gordon moved with effort. In recent weeks his arms and legs were quite useless.

The stranger, an older man, opened the car door for the woman within. Gordon smiled wryly: there was a man, perhaps twice his age, agilely performing what only months before had been his duties.

"My former employers didn't waste much time replacing me," said Gordon. "Well, I can't blame them."

The new driver assisted Mrs. Eldora Goodbond, smiling and cool-looking despite the city's July heat, from the car. She spoke to him briefly, then came lightly up the walk.

Gordon pulled himself up as best as he could, legs

drawn up as they were by the gradual paralysis that had benumbed his limbs. "Esther . . . " he began, and suddenly found that he had no voice. *"Esther . . ."* he whispered.

Lately, he had even suffered loss of sight and hearing at times. He covered his face with his hands in despair.

Outside, the man who had taken his place glanced at the sky with 20/20 vision and listened to the song of a sparrow.

After pleasant exchanges of greetings, Eldora Goodbond turned a steady gaze to Gordon. "I see you are no better, Worth."

"No, ma'am. Even the specialists have as much as said I'll never be well." He managed to speak hoarsely.

"He can't write anymore, can't straighten out his legs!" Esther exclaimed.

"And sometimes I can't even yell at my wife," said Gordon. "You'd better keep that new man out there. Looks as if I won't be chauffeuring for anybody, ever again."

"Worth, listen to me. You've heard us discussing the psychic readings of Edgar Cayce."

Respectful silence.

"Well, I've asked for a reading for you. It's scheduled for September 11."

Gordon sighed heavily. "Yes, ma'am."

"You don't seem very excited. He's helped *us* through several illnesses, as you know."

Esther moved closer and took his hand. "We have no money to pay for a reading," she said.

"I have arranged for Worth's expenses, including his transportation."

Doubt mixed with gratitude in Gordon. "Thank you, Mrs. Goodbond. I'll repay you if ever I can." Inwardly, he thought, *I just don't believe, I can't believe!*

Esther found work in a dress shop so that they could maintain their modest home. Gordon's mother, who

188

lived nearby, had come in to help care for him. About all she could do, however, was to administer the sedatives prescribed by his doctors.

His reading was given on September 11, as planned. They received word from Miss Gladys Davis that he was to be admitted to the hospital on October 5.

At the train station two black porters stepped from the southbound train to the platform. One of them, a rather large man, spotted Gordon as he was being helped from the limousine by the new chauffeur and another porter. The concerned black man came over and said, "I b'lieve I can carry him right to his berth."

Like a mother, he then gathered Gordon into his long arms, and Gordon grinned. "Now *that's* service!" he said as he was hoisted from the platform onto the train. There was an awkward moment as they turned through the narrow passage into the waiting train car. Then the porter was bearing Gordon, who weighed 140 pounds, to a lower berth.

"Just let me know if I can be of any more service, sir," said the smiling fellow.

"Thanks," Gordon nodded. Esther tipped him. To himself, he said, *I wonder if Gordon Worth can be of any more service?*

As the train pulled out of the station and Esther slipped from view, he began to ponder what his reading had said at the end: something about service—that without service to others, one could gain little.

Then why had God taken away his very power to serve?

First, there had been his replacement, the "old man" who was now the Goodbonds' chauffeur. Now, he had been obliged to be carried like a baby by the kindly black porter . . . How he envied them both!

He lay quietly, submitting to the lull of the train's motion. He remembered the time when his body was young and strong. He had been sure of everything, taking life itself for granted. But what had the reading said? It had said that life itself was a *service*.

The thought was sinking into his consciousness as he fell asleep.

The next day, he was whisked from the Norfolk station out to Virginia Beach and up to his room. As he was wheeled to his bed, he was reassured by the cheerfulness and tidiness of the staff and the hospital itself. Treatment was begun at once.

His condition was very good in some respects, his reading had stated. He was warned that further inroads into his system would be harder to combat if not checked. The pain relievers he had been taking were probably what Cayce was referring to by the phrase "outside influence" which had "caused derangements in his system which prevented proper distribution of that assimilated."

In studying Gordon's case Lyman Lydic, D.O., meticulously followed the prescribed treatment. Osteopathy, diet, and mental suggestion were foremost: "proper resuscitating forces as may be guided by the inner man itself, through that of the mental and physical coordinating together."

Before diagnosing Gordon's entire condition, Cayce began the reading with: "Now, we find the conditions are abstruse in some respects as respecting the physical forces of the body. While in many respects conditions are very good, there are those conditions in the physical that, taking warning of in the present, will prevent further inroads or later developments as would be much *harder* to combat than that as has been existent through this inactivity of that assimilated in its proper sphere or manner."

Characteristically, Cayce diagnosed Gordon's entire state, finding the blood to be below normal. In the nerves he found "impingements in the cerebrospinal system as produced by exterior influences and the result of the bacilli as has been active—or was active in the system, especially in those centers just below the solar plexus, or that of the 9th, 10th, and 11th dorsal—these not only being for a cold internal system, as related to the assimilating forces of the system, but to the locomotory system those of a disturbance between the sympathetic and cerebrospinal, in the lower lumbar plexus.

"This prevents proper coordination in the sympathetic and cerebrospinal and makes for the activities in the lower portion of the body, becoming those of voluntary-involuntary in their reflex."

Reflexes to the sensory system led to improper reflexes in throat, hearing, and eyes. "In the functioning of the organs, themselves—This as has been seen or given—these are very good, save as to the reflexes to the sensory system which, being in that position of incoordination between the sympathetic and cerebrospinal in the lower portion—makes for, in the cervical and those of the hypogastric and pneumogastric plexus, as they cross in the upper portion of the body, those reflexes that make for the over-activity, or an accentuation of the functioning of the organs, as is seen at times from the throat—or in voice and speech; at others in the hearing, again as seen from the eyes. *All* of these, in their respective cycle, *have* had, or *do* have, their improper reflexes."

Dr. Lydic began a program of weekly osteopathic correction with massage as prescribed: two general treatments to one adjustment. The corrective one was in the cerebrospinal system, lumbar, and dorsal regions; the general, from the solar plexus upward.

The sinusidal reaction, a form of electro-therapy, would make for the high, not the low, vibration. It was to be administered in specific areas "making same conjunctive with that of the brachial centers, or in the 2nd and 3rd dorsal, and those of the lower portion of the lumbar, or that in the 4th and in the 1st sacral. These would be changed, to be sure, for a *direct* reaction—after there has begun to be adjustments made, and the application then would be of the 3rd and 4th cervical, and to the umbilicus plexus—just *below* the umbilicus. These would make for a direct reaction, which will change for the vibrations through those of the intestinal system, so that assimilations are in accord with the vibrations of the body, so that the blood supply and the blood building becomes the nearer normal in its reaction; taking also, internally, those of the properties as would be in compound, as in this. . . ." There followed a prescription which included distilled water, ambrosia leaves, prickly ash bark, dog-fennel or Mayblossom, and wild ginseng. This was to be reduced by simmering to one-half the quantity, strained, and added to 35 per cent alcohol, balsam of tolu, and tincture of Capsici.

This was to be taken in very small doses: half a tea-spoon four times a day, twenty minutes before meals.

Diet was particularly important in Gordon's case. He was to have citrus fruits often for breakfast, in addition to oat meal or Wheatena, although Cayce warned else-where they should not be taken in the same meal with citrus.

Noon meals were to consist principally of raw veg-etables, especially celery, lettuce, and tomatoes. Oil dress-ings with tapioca would aid digestion.

Evening meals were to include fish or juices of meats; well-cooked vegetables, using the peelings of white po-tatoes; yams or turnips rather than the pulp usually served. Iron was to be gained from spinach and kale, well-cooked, without any grease except butter.

Eliminations were to be aided mainly by his diet.

Then Cayce urged coordinating mental and physical healing. The one administering to Gordon, Dr. Lydic, should do so "in a gentle, quiet, easy way and manner. Blustering about the individual will only irritate. To scold, or to be too much of the commanding nature, is to destroy the better portion of that that may be builded in the body. Learn, or train the body—not only to be good, but be good *for* something. Let there be known there is a duty to self, and hope in service—for without service to the other, one may gain little in this experience in life's forces; for Life Itself *is* a service. *Use,* not abuse."

Finding such words were meant for *him,* finding the staff, Dr. Lydic, and Edgar Cayce himself taking a personal interest in him, Gordon responded gratefully. As he was benefitted by the healing service of others, he opened his mind and heart to be healed. To Gordon's brother-in-law, Edgar Cayce was later to write, "We all came to love Mr. Worth when he was here . . ."

Within one week, Gordon began responding dramatically to his treatment. He felt once more that his hands and arms were a part of him; his command over them returned to such an extent he was able to write letters home telling the good news. He was elated.

Within that same week, he struggled one day from his bed and found he had the use of his legs, however weak; he tottered with some amazement to the bathroom.

On October 14, a second reading was given. "There are changes in the physical forces of the body, as is indicated by the better use of the limbs, of the changes in the eliminations, and in the distribution of that as is assimilated. In the releasing of the pressures as have been apparent in the lumbar, the sacral, and especially the coccyx, we will find that nerve energy to extremities will be more active in its activities in the physical functioning of the body."

Cayce now advised saturated solutions or packs of epsom salts; after osteopathic treatments, Gordon should be exposed to violet ray.

"How long before improvement will be noticed in legs?" was asked.

"In eight to twelve days."

On October 19, Eldora Goodbond wrote: "We are so glad Worth is making such wonderful progress. I think his case is an interesting one for the Hospital. Doctors have admitted their inability to help and his cure will be a comparatively fast one."

Sure enough, three weeks from the time he was admitted to the hospital, he was well enough to leave. He still needed treatment. "I was not well," he wrote to this writer in 1970, "but the hospital was uncertain, everyone talking of closing. Dr. Lydic left before I did."

The hospital was indeed going through anxious days. It was only a matter of months before it closed, following the stock market failure and its aftermath.

When Gordon stepped off the train in the city, the same porter was there to meet him. The porter's eyes rounded in disbelief. Then he broke out in great smiles. "You're walking!"

"With a cane, but I'm walking!"

Treatment was continued under Theodore Berger, D.O., during the winter of 1930–31, under the Goodbond's sponsorship.

"I am glad to tell you I am still gaining," Gordon wrote Edgar Cayce. "I weigh 170 . . . I can walk about a mile in a day, but of course I get awful tired . . ."

In his third reading, given December 1, Cayce stated that Gordon was still showing improvement. He was to have only one general osteopathic treatment a week and one massage with balsam of sulphur in the lumbar and sacral regions, being rubbed thoroughly along the limbs to the knees and ankles, as well as the hips. The masseuse was to follow the course of the muscles rather than the nerves. "We will find that more of the greater strength will be gained by the body through this mode of application. This may be given by any masseuse, or by one at home—will it be *thoroughly* done, see?

"Keep up the general diet as has been outlined.

"Exercise in the open as much as possible, but do not overtax nor strain self, and it will be found that in an earlier period than expected the body will be able to return to daily labors—or work—as is desired."

On February 9, Gordon, having continued on this basis, wrote that he was sending for a mental, physical, and spiritual reading. "I can never thank you enough for all you have done for me and I am sure I will continue to gain. Also I can never repay Mrs. Goodbond for getting my first reading and telling me about you."

He still had some numbness in his limbs, too quick pulsation, dizziness, congestion of the liver. This last was due to the liver "adjusting itself to the manner in which administrations for aid have been given, with cold making it more acute at times." Cayce prescribed a vegetable compound such as Castoria or syrup of figs for stirring the liver. Increased manipulations would also help.

His circulation was improving constantly. He was actually concerned with gaining weight too fast, so that Cayce replied to this question that he should leave off starches and, for the next 30 to 40 days, keep a diet restricted to lamb, nerve-building fruits, pineapple. He was to have no butter, taking everything in as near its normal state as possible without the addition of sugar. He was to have no potatoes of any kind. He was to decrease the refill of his prescription until it was gone. Gordon was to follow the work he had found to be in keeping with his natural tendencies.

"Will body's health be so can safely have children, and when?" Gordon asked.

"This, we find, will be better, so that the body may *beget* children, in an early portion of the present year— or in the latter portion of present year."

"Any advice regarding mental or spiritual body?"

"As the body has builded in the mental forces, this recuperation has begun. Keep an ideal and work towards same."

Gordon now recommended Cayce to his brother-in-law, who wrote Cayce to thank him for helping both Gordon and his own mother. "He (Gordon) is fine, working every day, and always talking about you."

As soon as he could manage it (May 5, 1931) Gordon was back at work on the Goodbonds' estate, seven months after starting treatment with Cayce.

Dr. Berger wrote in June: ". . . in my opinion it is the most spectacular cure that has ever been effected through the readings. He was a helpless, hopeless cripple and is now doing hard, physical labor on the Goodbond place . . ."

In his own report, Gordon wrote: "I am writing this letter in appreciation for all you did for me . . . have not laid off one day since [going back to work] . . . I tell everyone how Mr. Cayce helped me . . . You can show this letter to anyone to prove the good you can do by your readings. As you know, when people first hear about a reading they cannot believe in it. I did not at first and I hope others who are sick will let you help them before waiting too long."

Esther and Gordon had a son born to them in 1933 and another in 1937. Together, they have built a successful farming enterprise. Today, Gordon Worth looks back and calls his cure "a miracle."

Medical Commentary: Paralysis

by William A. McGarey, M.D.

Gordon was only twenty-two years old when this strange paralysis began in his body. He must have wondered—as apparently his doctors did—just what in the world was causing him to become a hopeless cripple with spastic legs, useless arm, at times unable to see or hear or talk. For a young man in the prime years of his early manhood, having held down a responsible job as a chauffeur, the frustration, the fear of disability must have been intense.

Perhaps it was this underlying emotional pattern that caused Cayce to put such strong emphasis on the manner in which Gordon was to be handled psychologically by those caring for him and, likewise, on the attitudes which the patient himself was instructed to develop.

There is no question today that we can shape our emotional patterns; that these patterns, which activated, are wholly consistent with the hormonal activity of our endocrine glands; and that hormone levels have a vital, irreplaceable role to play in any normal regeneration activity within the basic cellular structure of the human body.

Gordon apparently was receptive to the advice given him and was also apparently what we would think of as a sensitive, retentive individual—the type of person who would respond best to suggestions of a constructive nature. The admonition to him that all of life is a service must have struck a responsive chord and probably made possible the full rehabilitation that eventually came about.

The part of this story, however, that catches my medical fancy most grippingly is the paralysis itself—the nature of its inception, as Cayce described it, and the manner in which the repair process might come about.

As a general practitioner, I have not seen a large number of severe neurological problems. Today they usually end up in the hands of the neurologist or neurosurgeon. It would have been very helpful, in my opinion and for my purposes, if Gordon could have had a neurological workup to establish just what type of lesion, in the medical world of nomenclature, Cayce was dealing with.

There are dozens of different syndromes described in the neurology textbooks in which a condition has been observed often enough and identified sufficiently that it has been given a name. Often the name is that of the person who first described it as an entity, but the exact cause and the curative therapy program both often remain a mystery. Some of these conditions recover in a manner we call "spontaneous." This means that the body brings about its own healing process in a manner we do not understand, or we would have aided the body in its activity.

Several years ago, I treated a man whose paralysis of the legs was determined by my neurological consultant to be a Guillain-Barre's syndrome or disease. You can look this term up in a convenient neurological textbook or medical dictionary. This patient was in his fifties, and the problem developed gradually. He did not have any spasticity, however, and he had no real sensory symptoms. It was caught fairly early, and a vigorous program of physical therapy, massage, and diet brought about a gradual restoration to his continued activity as a college professor. Gordon's difficulty did not fit this picture.

The problem Gordon had might be diagnosed from the story by a good neurologist; but to me, at least, this was a syndrome which, without therapy, would have made of the patient a lifelong cripple, with life expectancy markedly reduced. There seems to be little question of that.

But Cayce looked inside the body, saw pressures on nerve structures, saw deficiencies in nerve plexuses that needed replenishing, and could identify forces of the body that control the locomotory system of the body. Cayce saw incoordination as an individual affect between the cerebrospinal and the autonomic nervous systems of the body. As a psychic who could lie down and enter what we call an extended state of consciousness, Cayce could clairvoyantly look at these functions and forces and deficiencies much as we look at noses and ears and abdomens.

If indeed some of these rare neurological conditions are related in their etiology or in their abnormal physiology; if incoordination, lack of proper assimilation, pressures, and deficiencies are part and parcel of each; and if Cayce's clairvoyant qualities were accurate, we would have a thesis and an hypothesis upon which to build a system of rehabilitation that could turn some of the Gordons of this world into active, contributing members of society rather than the cripples that they may find themselves.

What *did* Cayce see about this young fellow and his inner workings?

He pointed out that there had been in times past an infection—or bacilli—present in the blood stream. This, plus other undescribed "external influences," had created impingements on the nerves of the cerebrospinal system arising in the ninth, tenth, and eleventh dorsal segments. As in all disease processes, one thing leads to another. Cayce saw two abnormalities arising from these impingements:

1. A "cold internal system" as related to the entire process of assimilation in the body. I would assume he meant here the actual temperature of the stomach, esophagus, duodenum, spleen, liver, pancreas, and small intestine was actually below normal. This produced in turn a lack of proper substances, necessary for normal body sustenance, taken from the food. In other words, the body was being partially or specifically starved. This needed to be alleviated or a worse condition would develop.

2. An incoordination between the functioning of the cerebrospinal and the autonomic nervous systems. In hundreds of other readings Cayce described this condition as arising because of pressures in those areas where the two systems have their channels of communication —the recurrent branches of nerves at each spinal segment which connect the spinal cord to the sympathetic ganglia. When the impulses flowing through these nerves are disturbed in their nature, frequency, or force, an incoordination comes about which might bring into being a variety of conditions, dependent on the state of being of the rest of the body.

In this particular case, nervous system incoordination created again two conditions:

1. A lower lumbar plexus incoordination as it affected the locomotory system, or simple muscular action in the legs. Cayce said it like this: This incoordination "makes for the activities in the lower portion of the body becoming those of voluntary-involuntary in their reflex" (a beautiful description of the spasticity found throughout the lower part of the body).

2. An effect in the sensory apparatus in its reflexes, in the eyes, ears, voice. Cayce saw the sensory nervous

system as a unit in itself—in a true sense apart from the autonomic or cerebrospinal. Thus the voice, as related to that which hears the voice, is also a part of the sensory nervous system. He also described the sensory system as being more closely related in its reflexes to the autonomic nervous system than to the brain itself. This attitude is upheld by our observations of the manner in which the sound of music, for instance, can have a quieting effect on the feelings of a sensitive person and how one using words can induce hypnotically far-reaching physiological effects throughout the body. The touchstone soothes a person's disturbed feelings. The erotic picture, through the visual apparatus, brings about a sudden conditioned autonomic response. The examples are almost numberless in their variety.

Cayce described the incoordination here as bringing about an effect which is better quoted for its full impact:

In the functioning of the organs themselves—this, as has been seen or given—these are very good, save as to the reflexes to the *sensory* system, which—being in that position of incoordination between the sympathetic and cerebrospinal in the lower portion—makes for, in the cervical and those of the hypogastric and pneumogastric plexus, as they cross in the upper portion of the body, those reflexes that make for the over-activity, or an accentuation of the functioning of the organs, as is seen at times from the throat—or in voices and speech; at others in the hearing, again as seen from the eyes. *All* of those, in their respective cycles, *have* had, or *do* have, their improper reflexes. (53-1)

Cayce also described certain activities within the body that we do not as yet relate to causation or therapy, probably because we have not yet accepted them at the conscious level.

From Gordon's reading comes the suggestion that there are radial forces within the body that supply from certain centers the replenishing in the nerve and blood forces of the limbs or the extremities "in their activity." These centers are the lumbar and solar plexuses, especially, and they apparently radiate their activity through locomotory centers existing in various parts of the spinal cord. Whether this radiation is through the nervous system pathways or by a vibratory route through the finer vibratory body of the individual was not clarified in this reading. In other data found in the readings, however, the nature of the "vibratory body" was more fully discussed.

The key to recovery from this strange complex of conditioning appeared to be the supplying to the body the "incentives" in order that certain portions might respond in a way that would build the defective portions of the body. Balance, coordination, health, and strength might once again be the experience of the afflicted person. Cayce realized that some dietary suggestions had been followed and some manipulative procedures had been accomplished. Nevertheless, he added:

> . . . both of these, as we find, have been neglected in part; for with the releasing of pressures, unless there are the incentives given as would cause or produce a resuscitation of the forces as regulate the activity of the extremities— especially in the lumbar or solar plexus centers, radiating through those of the locomotories—these will *not*, just because the pressure is taken off at times, build—*without* that as would stimulate same *to* the point where there may be resuscitation for those centers where impingements have existed, and where there is still the lack of proper filling or supplying of nutriment for the proper activities. (53-1)

We find Cayce's therapy program designed to bring about a regeneration of the nerve forces and centers, a reactivation of the assimilation, and a gradual restoration of the physical body through:

1. Manipulation and massage
2. Dietary regime

3. Incentives given to the body in various ways: sinusoidal electrotherapy; ultraviolet treatments; violet ray therapy; suggestion therapy; Ginsengherbal mixture; epsom salts packs to the sacrum; balsam of sulfur rubs to the sacral and lumbar areas and down over the muscular pathways of the extremities; and exercise.

It is a complex story of physiological balances to be maintained while building up the total functional capacity of the body, but isn't it fascinating? And does it not give one the feeling that we are on the threshold of finding new ways (or are they actually regained out of the records of antiquity?) to bring healing to the body, hope to the mind, and direction to the spirit of man on the earth?

Gordon had a right to be enthusiastic about his recovery—much as we have a right to be enthusiastic about healing the ills of mankind. Gordon learned, perhaps, the meaning of service.

THE A.R.E. TODAY

The Association for Research and Enlightenment, Inc., is a non-profit, open membership organization committed to spiritual growth, holistic healing, psychical research and its spiritual dimensions; and more specifically, to making practical use of the psychic readings of the late Edgar Cayce. Through nationwide programs, publications and study groups, A.R.E. offers all those interested, practical information and approaches for individual study and application to better understand and relate to themselves, to other people and to the universe. A.R.E. membership and outreach is concentrated in the United States with growing involvement throughout the world.

The headquarters at Virginia Beach, Virginia, include a library/conference center, administrative offices and publishing facilities, and are served by a beachfront motel. The library is one of the largest metaphysical, parapsychological libraries in the country. A.R.E. operates a bookstore, which also offers mail-order service and carries approximately 1,000 titles on nearly every subject related to spiritual growth, world religions, parapsychology and transpersonal psychology. A.R.E. serves its members through nationwide lecture programs, publications, a Braille library, a camp and an extensive Study Group Program.

The A.R.E. facilities, located at 67th Street and Atlantic Avenue, are open year-round. Visitors are always welcome and may write A.R.E., P.O. Box 595, Virginia Beach, VA 23451, for more information about the Association.